How to use Read & Respond in your classroom...

Read & Respond provides teaching ideas related to a specific well-loved children's book. Each Read & Respond book is divided into the following sections:

ABOUT THE BOOK AND AUTHOR

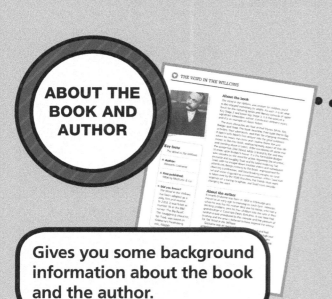

Gives you some background information about the book and the author.

GUIDED READING

Breaks the book down into sections and gives notes for using it with guided reading groups. A bookmark has been provided on page 12 containing comprehension questions. The children can be directed to refer to these as they read.

SHARED READING

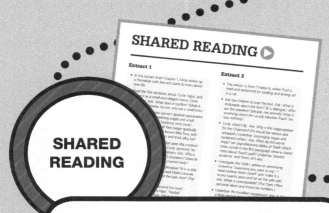

Provides extracts from the children's book with associated notes for focused work. There is also one non-fiction extract that relates to the children's book.

GRAMMAR, PUNCTUATION & SPELLING

Provides word-level work related to the children's book so you can teach grammar, punctuation and spelling in context.

SCHOLASTIC
READ & RESPOND

Bringing the best books to life in the classroom

Activities based on The Wind in the Willows By Kenneth Grahame

FOR AGES 7–11

Scholastic Education, an imprint of Scholastic Ltd
Book End, Range Road, Witney, Oxfordshire, OX29 0YD
Registered office: Westfield Road, Southam, Warwickshire CV47 0RA

Printed and bound by Ashford Colour Press
© 2019 Scholastic Ltd
1 2 3 4 5 6 7 8 9 9 0 1 2 3 4 5 6 7 8

British Library Cataloguing-in-Publication Data
A catalogue record for this book is available from the British Library.
ISBN 978-1407-18247-6

Extracts from *The National Curriculum in England, English Programme of Study* © Crown Copyright. Reproduced under the terms of the Open Government Licence (OGL). http://www.nationalarchives.gov.uk/doc/open-government-licence/version/3

Due to the nature of the web, we cannot guarantee the content or links of any site mentioned. We strongly recommend that teachers check websites before using them in the classroom.

Authors Eileen Jones
Editorial team Rachel Morgan, Vicki Yates, Suzanne Adams, Julia Roberts
Series designers Neil Salt and Alice Duggan
Designer Alice Duggan
Illustrator Mike Phillips/ Beehive Illustration

Acknowledgements
The publishers gratefully acknowledge permission to reproduce the following copyright material:
Scholastic Children's Books for permission to use the cover from *The Wind in the Willows* written by Kenneth Grahame (Scholastic Children's Books, 2014). Reproduced with permission of Scholastic Children's Books. All rights reserved.

Every effort has been made to trace copyright holders for the works reproduced in this book, and the publishers apologise for any inadvertent omissions.

PLOT, CHARACTER & SETTING ▶

1. Setting off

Objectives
To predict what might happen from details stated and implied

What you need
Copies of *The Wind in the Willows*, photocopiable page 29 'Setting off'

What to do
- Use this activity after reading Chapter 1.
- Remind the children that a story has three strands: setting, character and plot. Explain that setting includes time and place. Point out the mention of spring, seasonal changes and the state of the countryside and river bank in Chapter 1. Read about descriptions of the scenery on Mole and Rat's boating trip and the chapter's final sentence.
- Ask: What does Mole hear/smell whispering through the reeds? Ask: Does setting seem important in this book? What places could Mole explore?
- Ask: Who do you think is the main character here? Why? Agree that the chapter begins and ends with Mole's actions. Comment on 'emancipated' in the final paragraph. Ask: What does it mean? What does it suggest? Is Mole going to stay on the river?
- Discuss the plot. Ask: Has much happened? Share ideas, identifying Mole's exploration, discovery of a river and friendship with Rat. Ask: Are there other animals for Mole to befriend?
- Give out photocopiable page 29 'Setting off'. Ask the children to jot down their observations and predictions drawn from Chapter 1, dividing them into setting, characters and plot.

Differentiation
Extension: Ask children to justify their ideas with references to the text.

2. Ducks' Ditty

Objective
To prepare poems and plays to read aloud and to perform, showing understanding through intonation, tone and volume so that the meaning is clear to an audience.

What you need
Copies of *The Wind in the Willows*

What to do
- After reading Chapter 1, direct the children to Rat's composition at the beginning of the chapter. Ask: What is a ditty? (a short, simple song)
- Read the first verse aloud. Define 'dabbling' (getting wet every so often by putting their heads into the water). Indicate the visual image 'Yellow feet a-quiver'. Ask: What do the words show about Rat? (his observation of the river)
- Put the children into small discussion groups to investigate the song's construction. Ask: What do you notice about the verses? (a rhyme scheme) Are punctuation and repetition important?
- Share results, indicating the separate first verse and the repetition of the following three. Identify the regular rhyme pattern, occasional exclamation marks and repetition of 'dabbling' and 'Up tails all'. Ask: Is Rat emphasising these actions?
- Suggest that a song is meant to be heard. Create four groups and assign each group a verse of 'Ducks' Ditty' to rehearse. The children must consider tone, speed, emphasis and volume. Encourage them to think about whether they will all perform each line or build the speakers towards the end.
- Let each group perform in order, and ask listeners to consider how the words affect their attitude to the ducks and river life.

READ&RESPOND The Wind in the Willows 29

PLOT, CHARACTER & SETTING

Contains activity ideas focused on the plot, characters and the setting of the story.

GET WRITING

Provides writing activities related to the children's book. These activities may be based directly on the children's book or be broadly based on the themes and concepts of the story.

TALK ABOUT IT

Has speaking and listening activities related to the children's book. These activities may be based directly on the children's book or be broadly based on the themes and concepts of the story.

ASSESSMENT

Contains short activities that will help you assess whether the children have understood concepts and curriculum objectives. They are designed to be informal activities to feed into your planning.

> The titles are great fun to use and cover exactly the range of books that children most want to read. It makes it easy to explore texts fully and ensure the children want to keep on reading more.
>
> *Chris Flanagan, Year 5 Teacher,*
> *St Thomas of Canterbury*
> *Primary School*

Activities

The activities follow the same format:

- **Objective:** the objective for the lesson. It will be based upon a curriculum objective, but will often be more specific to the focus being covered.

- **What you need:** a list of resources you need to teach the lesson, including photocopiable pages.

- **What to do:** the activity notes.

- **Differentiation:** this is provided where specific and useful differentiation advice can be given to support and/or extend the learning in the activity. Differentiation by providing additional adult support has not been included as this will be at a teacher's discretion based upon specific children's needs and ability, as well as the availability of support.

The activities are numbered for reference within each section and should move through the text sequentially – so you can use the lesson while you are reading the book. Once you have read the book, most of the activities can be used in any order you wish.

⬇ CURRICULUM LINKS

Section	Activity	Curriculum objectives
Guided reading		Comprehension: To predict what might happen from details stated and implied.
Shared reading	1	Comprehension: To draw inferences such as inferring characters' feelings, thoughts and motives from their actions, and to justify inferences with evidence.
	2	Comprehension: To check that the text makes sense to them, discussing their understanding and exploring the meaning of words in context.
	3	Comprehension: To discuss and evaluate how writers use language, including figurative language, considering the impact on the reader.
	4	Comprehension: To retrieve... information from non-fiction; to identify how structure and presentation contribute to meaning.
Grammar, punctuation & spelling	1	Composition: To ensure correct subject and verb agreement when using singular and plural; to proofread for spelling and punctuation errors.
	2	Composition: To link ideas across paragraphs.
	3	Vocabulary, grammar and punctuation: To use brackets, dashes or commas to indicate parenthesis.
	4	Composition: To ensure the consistent and correct use of tense throughout a piece of writing.
	5	Vocabulary, grammar and punctuation: To use hyphens to avoid ambiguity.
	6	Composition: To use a wide range of devices to build cohesion within and across paragraphs.
Plot, character & setting	1	Comprehension: To predict what might happen from details stated and implied.
	2	Spoken Language: To prepare poems and plays to read aloud and to perform, showing understanding through intonation, tone and volume so that the meaning is clear to an audience.
	3	Comprehension: To draw inferences, such as inferring characters' feelings, thoughts and motives from their actions, and to justify inferences with evidence.
	4	Comprehension: To read books that are structured in different ways.
	5	Comprehension: To identify and discuss themes and conventions in... a wide range of writing.
	6	Comprehension: To discuss and evaluate how authors use language, considering the impact on the reader.
	7	Comprehension: To check that the book makes sense to them... exploring the meaning of words in context; to draw inferences.
	8	Comprehension: To draw inferences, such as inferring characters' feelings, thoughts and motives from their actions, and to justify inferences with evidence.

Section	Activity	Curriculum objectives
Talk about it	**1**	Spoken language: To give well-structured... narratives for different purposes, including for expressing feelings.
	2	Spoken language: To consider and evaluate different viewpoints.
	3	Spoken language: To participate in discussions and debates.
	4	Spoken language: To use spoken language to develop understanding through speculating, hypothesising, imagining and exploring ideas.
	5	Spoken language: To participate in... role play. Comprehension: To infer characters' feelings, thoughts and motives.
	6	Spoken language: To use spoken language to develop understanding through speculating, hypothesising, imagining and exploring ideas.
Get writing	**1**	Composition: To précis longer passages.
	2	Composition: To perform their own compositions, using appropriate intonation, volume and movement so that meaning is clear.
	3	Composition: To identify the audience for and purpose of the writing, selecting the appropriate form and using other similar writing as models for their own.
	4	Composition: To select appropriate grammar and vocabulary, understanding how such choices can change and enhance meaning.
	5	Composition: To write narratives, describing settings, characters and atmosphere and integrating dialogue to convey character and advance the action.
	6	Composition: To use further organisational devices to structure text and to guide the reader.
Assessment	**1**	Composition: To note and develop initial ideas, drawing on reading and research where necessary.
	2	Composition: To describe settings, characters and atmosphere and integrate dialogue to convey character and advance the action.
	3	Comprehension: To check that the book makes sense to them, discussing their understanding and exploring the meaning of words in context.
	4	Comprehension: To identify and discuss themes and conventions across a wide range of writing.
	5	Comprehension: To ask questions to improve their understanding.
	6	Composition: To assess the effectiveness of their own and others' writing.

Key facts

The Wind in the Willows

⦿ **Author:**
Kenneth Grahame

⦿ **First published:**
1908 by Methuen & Co.

⦿ **Did you know?**
The Wind in the Willows has been adapted as a play, film and musical. In 2003, it was listed as number 16 in the BBC survey 'The Big Read'. The swaggering character, Mr Toad, was based on Grahame's headstrong son, Alastair.

About the book

The Wind in the Willows was written for children, but it is also enjoyed immensely by adults. As such, it is an ideal book for the maturing tastes and literacy curricula of upper Key Stage 2 and lower Key Stage 3. It is the work of a significant Edwardian author; it embraces different styles; and it is an example of classic fiction.

The main characters are four animal friends: Mole, Rat, Badger and Toad. The book describes their quiet day-to day activities, their adventures, and their life-changing moments. It opens with Mole's first venture into the great outdoors where he meets the clever and creative Water Rat and moves to the river bank, embracing every aspect of river life and messing about in boats. After wandering off alone into the dangerous Wild Wood, Mole is found by Rat and they stumble upon Badger's house. It is the formidable Badger who decides on the need for action regarding the eccentric, excitable and naughty Toad and his latest motoring fad. Toad, with his escape down knotted sheets and subsequent adventures, brings comedy to the book: imprisonment for cheeking a policeman, and breath-taking escapes on land, rail and water disguised as a washerwoman. When Toad Hall is taken over by the Wild Wooders, the friends must work together on a daring recapture, and Toad must consider changing his ways.

About the author

Kenneth Grahame was born in 1859 in Edinburgh and moved at an early age to Inveraray on Loch Fyne. However, when he was five his mother died and his father, who had a drinking problem, sent his four children into the care of their grandmother in Cookham Dean, Berkshire. It was here that Grahame was introduced to the riverside and the pleasure of boating and the area is believed to have inspired the setting for *The Wind in the Willows*.

Grahame was an outstanding pupil at school and had ambitions to attend Oxford University, however the high cost meant it was beyond his reach. Instead, in 1879, he began working at the Bank of England, where he stayed until 1908 when he retired due to ill-health.

On retirement, Grahame, his wife and his son, Alastair, moved back to Cookham. Grahame had already had short stories and books published, but it was in Cookham and on his boating holidays without his family, that he turned Alastair's bedtime stories into his masterpiece, *The Wind in the Willows*. Kenneth Grahame died in 1932.

GUIDED READING ▶

Chapter 1: The River Bank

Refer to the book's title before reading Chapter 1. Ask: *Where do 'willows' grow?* (near water) Explore the quick start, contrasting Mole's irritated, underground weariness with his joyful, outdoor energy. Ask: *What changes him?* (sunlight) Identify 'pettishly' and ask: *Why does he change again?* (The river divides them.) Compare the knowledgeable Rat with the innocent Mole. Indicate 'nervously' when Mole hears 'Wild Wood'. Ask: *Which animals is even Rat wary of?* ('Weasels – and stoats – and foxes – and so on.') Comment on Mole's constant delight at river pleasures and his awareness of 'animal-etiquette'. Ask: *Why does the boat overturn?* (Mole tries to row.) Discuss the meaning of 'emancipated' in the final paragraph. Ask: *How does Rat contribute to this freedom?* (He teaches Mole water skills.) Discuss question 1 on the Guided reading bookmark as you consider the link between the final lines and the book's title. Ask the children to discuss question 9 on the bookmark.

Chapter 2: The Open Road

Read Chapter 2, commenting on developments since Chapter 1: Mole's confidence in water ('Since early morning he had been swimming in the river') and his relaxed openness with 'Ratty'. Recall references to Toad in Chapter 1. Ask: *How did he sound?* (unusual) *Does Toad's home confirm this?* Identify 'mellowed red brick', 'Toad Hall', 'boathouse', 'stables', 'banqueting-hall', 'flower-decked lawns'. Define 'fad'. (craze) Comment on the exclamation marks in Toad's speech. *What do they suggest?* (liveliness) Compare Mole's enthusiasm for the caravan with Rat's detachment. Ask: *Why does Rat relent?* (He dislikes disappointing the other two.) Pick out 'triumphant'. *Does it suggest gloating?* Explore the effect of the car's appearance, speed and horn on Toad. Consider Rat's organisation skills in arranging the trip home. *What does the final line emphasise about Toad?* (impulsiveness and wealth) Ask the children to discuss question 7 on the bookmark.

Chapter 3: The Wild Wood

Read until 'the Terror of the Wild Wood!' Ask: *Why is Mole eager to meet Badger?* (He sounds important.) *What does 'evasively' suggest about Rat's true feelings about the Wild Wood?* (apprehension) *Why doesn't Rat stop Mole going alone?* (It is winter and Rat is asleep.) Comment on the speed at which light drains away once Mole enters the wood. Identify frightening sights and sounds: faces, whistling, pattering, the dashing rabbit's warning. Investigate growing panic as he runs 'aimlessly'.

Then read the rest of the chapter. Ask: *What proves that Rat recognises the Wood's dangers?* (He arms himself.) Explore Rat's intelligence and powers of deduction as he works out what Mole's cut means (they have found Badger's house). Comment on Rat's authority, taking action and giving instructions to secure safety. Direct the children to question 2 on the bookmark for discussion.

Chapter 4: Mr Badger

Read Chapter 4 together. Point out Badger's change of tone from 'gruff and suspicious' on recognising Rat and Mole. Read aloud the lengthy description of Badger's house. Use question 6 on the bookmark for class discussion. Comment on long sentences with multiple clauses and adjectives to match the intricate layout: 'tunnel-like passages… without apparent end'. Identify 'winked', 'smiled' and 'grinned'. Explain that the writer is using personification, treating objects as people. Point out the hedgehogs' deference to Mole and Rat: standing up when they enter, using 'sir'. Ask: *Does this signify lower status as well as youth?* Identify their non-Standard English ('me and little Billy') and limited vocabulary. Ask: *Why does Badger give Mole a personal tour? What do they share?* (They appreciate underground homes.) *Is Mole likely to avoid the Wild Wood in the future?*

Chapter 5: Dulce Domum

Ask: *What language is used in the chapter title?* Translate the Latin as 'sweet home'. Explain that Latin was more commonly taught in 1908. Read until 'The Rat stared straight…' and discuss together question 3 on the bookmark. Ask: *Why do Mole and Rat feel wistfulness?* (They are far from home.) *What summons does Mole feel as he walks on?* (the pull of his old home) Explore Mole's confused emotions: his old home calls, but he owes loyalty to Ratty.

Finish reading the chapter and investigate Mole's reaction to entering his old home. Contrast initial excitement with sad awareness of cramped shabbiness. Ask: *How does Rat put Mole at ease?* (He sees good in everything.) Identify Mole's pride when the field mice visit and Rat's determination that the occasion is a success. Direct the children to question 4 on the bookmark for discussion.

Chapter 6: Mr Toad

Read together until 'To my mind…'. Point out 'early part of summer'. Comment that seasonal changes are regularly linked to the animals' actions. Ask: *What is 'Toad's hour'?* (time to act about Toad's behaviour) Compare Mole's excitement with Badger and Rat's serious determination. Ask: *What ends Toad's cheerful welcome?* (stern silence from the others) Identify Badger's determined organisation, Mole and Rat's forceful action, and the collapse of Toad's bluster. Ask: *What fails to control Toad?* (talking) *What serious action follows?* (Toad is locked in.) Investigate Toad's manipulation of Rat with requests for a doctor and a lawyer. Ask: *How does Toad escape?* (He climbs down knotted sheets.) Identify repetition of 'as if in a dream'. Ask: *Does this make Toad's car theft seem more innocent?*

Read the rest of the chapter, contrasting the 'hapless', 'shrieking', 'miserable' Toad who is arrested and sentenced with Toad in the first part. *What is his most serious crime?* ('cheeking the police') Ask the children to discuss question 11 on the bookmark.

Chapter 7: The Piper at the Gates of Dawn

Compare this chapter title with Grahame's usual straightforward ones. Read the chapter together and identify the emphasis on river dangers (the weir and drowning). Comment that Mole is unusually assertive, suggesting the search. Ask: *What do they hear? How does it affect them?* (Distant piping calls them onward.) Investigate their progress to the weir and the island and what happens ('Awe', 'trembling violently'; the bearded creature with the baby otter, fear). Discuss together question 6 on the bookmark. Point out unexpected capital letters ('Nature's', 'Him', 'Presence'). *Do they suggest names of gods and spiritual beings? What is strange about Mole and Rat's conversation later?* (They return to earlier talk, forgetting what they have seen.) Read the song aloud, pointing out its repeated message: 'forget'. Encourage discussion of question 5 on the bookmark.

Chapter 8: Toad's Adventures

Read until 'With a quaking heart'. Point out Toad's assessments of his friends' characters. Ask: *Are they accurate?* Comment on Toad's short-lived humility. *What revives his spirit and appetite?* (the smell of hot cabbage) Ask: *Why is the gaoler's daughter attentive?* (She feels pity.) *What is Toad's interpretation?* (tender feelings for him) Indicate Toad's regret of a 'social gulf' and his sympathetic 'There, there' about a washerwoman aunt. *Does he feel superior? What is the plan for Toad's escape?* (He will dress as the washerwoman.)

Then read the rest of Chapter 8. Ask: *What goes wrong at the station?* (He is without pocket and contents.) Examine Toad's manipulation of the engine driver with his story of children waiting for him and his later plea. Ask: *What persuades the driver?* (He hates to see an animal in tears.) Identify Toad's quick mood change once off the train: laughter becomes misery on finding that he is lost, alone, cold and hungry. Discuss question 8 on the bookmark.

Chapter 9: Wayfarers All

Read Chapter 9 together, identifying the link between nature's 'change and departure' and Rat's restless mood. Ask: *Why are field mice too busy for a stroll or a picnic?* (They are planning winter quarters.) *What are the swallows discussing?* (winter migration) *What is the 'call of the South'?* (the summons of sunny warmth) Comment on Rat's unconvincing 'only life, to live'. *Has talking to others unsettled him?* Explore the wayfarer's tempting picture of places and travel. Ask: *How is Rat affected?* (His life feels 'somewhat narrow and circumscribed'.) *How does he respond to the wayfarer's invitation?* (He goes home and packs.) *What alarming physical change does Mole notice?* (Rat's eyes are the colour of the Wayfarer's.) Investigate Rat's strange state ('like a sleep-walker'; 'glazed and set' eyes; 'violent shivering'; 'hysterical fit of dry sobbing'; 'strange seizure'). Examine Mole's strength, care and thoughtful suggestion of poetry.

Chapter 10: The Further Adventures of Toad

Remind the children of Toad's whereabouts at the end of Chapter 8 and then read Chapter 10. Ask: *Why has Toad been comfortable enough?* (He is used to a prison floor.) Indicate 'Free!' *What does the repetition suggest?* (This matters most to Toad.) Point out Toad's quick reaction to a situation: he tells the barge owner a complicated story. *What mistake does he make?* (He brags conceitedly.) Ask: *What revenge does Toad take when thrown into the water?* (He takes the horse.) Comment on how quickly Toad spots another opportunity: selling the horse to the gypsy and feeding himself. Read his song aloud. Ask: *What is his main emotion?* (conceit) *What sends him into final despair?* (pursuit by the chauffeur and policemen) *Who looks likely to come to his rescue?* (Rat) Discuss question 10 on the bookmark.

Chapter 11: "Like Summer Tempests Came His Tears"

Read together Chapter 11, reminding the children of Toad's despair at the end of Chapter 10. Investigate his range of emotions as he talks to Rat: pride, remorse, sorrow, amused dismissal of friends' feelings, boastfulness. Explore how Toad, Rat and Mole talk at once, debating what to do. Ask: *What silences them?* (Badger's voice.) *Why do they react like this?* (respect) Point out Badger's understanding of Toad and how to treat him; links with his father; knowledge of the passage; plans for regaining Toad Hall. Comment on Mole's youthful naivety in revealing some plans. Ask: *Why does Badger praise Mole's foolishness? Is he pleased that the stoats will be 'nervous and flustered'?* Comment that this chapter is important because all four friends are together again. Discuss question 12 on the bookmark.

Chapter 12: The Return of Ulysses

Identify Ulysses as a returning hero in ancient Greek mythology. Ask: *Who is likely to be compared to Ulysses?* (Toad) Read the chapter and then comment on Toad's timidity and minor role in the secret passage. Ask: *Who leads the assault on the weasels?* (Badger) Examine the battle scene and the courage of all four friends. Ask: *How do they defeat so many weasels?* (Their noise, movement and apparent size makes the weasels panic.) Point out the special praise Badger gives Mole, and Toad's jealousy. Ask: *How does Toad eventually win praise from Badger?* (He thanks Mole.) Examine the effect on Toad of preparing for a banquet. *What is wrong with his invitations?* (They will lead to boasting.) Ask: *Who listens to Toad's last song?* (an imaginary audience) *Has Toad changed?*

The Wind in the Willows
by Kenneth Grahame

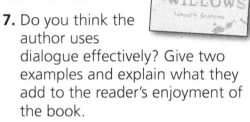

Focus on...
Meaning

1. Explain why the river is so important to the story. How does the book's title lead you to expect this?

2. Does the author present the River Rat as an appealing character? In what way? How is he treated by the other animals?

3. What predictions can you make about what may happen in the story from the title and early pages of this chapter?

4. Is Mole excited by his new 'upper life'? Does he regret leaving his underground home? Support your opinion with evidence from the text.

Focus on...
Organisation

5. How is the book organised? Is it an effective method? How does one chapter differ from another?

6. What devices does the author use here to build up atmosphere and information about the characters and the setting?

The Wind in the Willows
by Kenneth Grahame

Focus on...
Language and features

7. Do you think the author uses dialogue effectively? Give two examples and explain what they add to the reader's enjoyment of the book.

8. Identify words that suggest that *The Wind in the Willows* was written early in the 20th Century. What words might a modern writer use?

Focus on...
Purpose, viewpoints and effects

9. What is the purpose of this part of the story? Is it successful? Explain why you say this.

10. How does the author want you to regard Toad? Is he a rogue or a hero? What makes you think this?

11. Is the author making serious points here or is he just adding humour to the book? Supply evidence to support your opinion.

12. What lessons can the reader learn from the relationships between the four animals? Is one animal the hero of the book?

SHARED READING ▶

Extract 1

- In this extract from Chapter 1, Mole strikes up a friendship with Rat and starts to learn about river life.

- Read the first sentence aloud. Circle 'bijou' and define it as a small and elegant home. Circle 'dreamily'. Ask: *What does it confirm?* (Mole is imagining a home; he can only see a small hole.)

- Investigate the hole owner's gradual appearance by underlining 'something bright and small seemed to twinkle'; 'twinkled once more'; 'winked at him'; 'a small face began gradually to grow up round it'; 'A brown little face, with whiskers'; 'Small neat ears and thick silky hair'.

- Circle 'cautiously'. Ask: *What does this confirm?* (This is their first meeting.) Circle 'pettishly' for the children to supply a synonym. Ask: *Why is Mole reacting sulkily to Rat's invitation? Does he realise that the river can be crossed easily?*

- Circle 'talk'. Ask: *What is noticeable?* (It is in italic font.) Invite the children to read Mole's answer aloud. *What is the effect of the italic font?* (The word is emphasised.)

- Underline Rat's actions around the boat: 'stooped', 'unfastened a rope', 'hauled' and 'lightly stepped'. Ask: *What do they all reveal about him?* (boating competence and confidence)

- Underline 'whole heart went out to it' and 'rapture'. Ask: *How does Mole feel about boats?* (He is enthralled.)

Extract 2

- This extract is from Chapter 6, when Toad is tried and sentenced for stealing and driving off in a car.

- Ask the children to scan the text. Ask: *What is noticeable about the form?* (It is dialogue.) *Who are the speakers?* (people, not animals) *What is surprising about the usually talkative Toad?* (He says nothing.)

- Circle 'cheerfully'. Ask: *Why is this inappropriate for the Chairman?* (He should be serious and unbiased.) Underline 'incorrigible rogue and hardened ruffian'. Ask: *What do the words imply?* (an unprofessional dislike of Toad) *Which other words in the first paragraph show a closed mind about Toad's guilt?* Underline 'clearest evidence' and 'there isn't any''.

- Investigate the Clerk's advice on sentencing. Underline 'Supposing you were to say', 'I never believe more myself' and 'make it a round twenty years and be on the safe side'. Ask: *What is unacceptable?* (The Clerk offers personal views and imprecise numbers.)

- Underline 'An excellent suggestion!' Ask: *Is this a likely remark from a Chairman? What mood does the writer create?* (farcical) Read aloud the rest of the final paragraph. Ask: *Who is being spoken to?* Circle 'Prisoner!' and identify him as Toad. Underline 'Pull yourself together and try and stand up straight.' Ask: *What does this suggest about Toad's physical and emotional condition?* (collapsed and distraught)

- Underline: 'if you appear before us again… we shall have to deal with you very seriously!' Ask: *What is strange about this threat? Has Toad already been given a serious sentence? Do these words add humour to the text?*

Extract 3

- Taken from Chapter 12, this is part of the story's climax: the four friends recapture Toad Hall.

- Underline 'drew himself up'. Ask: *Why is the movement important?* (It emphasises Badger's size and decisiveness.) *How is strength suggested?* Underline 'firm grip' and 'both paws'.

- Read aloud the first three sentences of the sixth paragraph. Underline 'Well might' at the start of each. Ask: *What else do the three sentences have in common?* Circle the exclamation marks. *Why is the similar construction effective?* (It reinforces the chaos in the room.)

- Read aloud from 'They were but four' to the end of the paragraph. Circle the semicolon after 'cudgels', explaining that it separates the sentence's two clauses. Underline 'They were but four in all'. Ask: *Why are these words important?* (They stress the numerical difficulty of the battle.) Circle the word 'seemed'. Ask: *Why is it important? Do the four animals appear to the weasels and ferrets to be everywhere? How do the four achieve this?* (They are large, noisy, fast and heavily armed.)

- In a different colour, underline the final clause of the penultimate paragraph. Ask: *What contrast does the writer create?* (In spite of large numbers, the numerous weasels and ferrets are cowardly; the four friends are heroic.)

- Circle 'Heroes' and 'Friends' in the final two paragraphs. Ask: *Why are capital letters used?* (They award a special status.) Ask: *What is emphasised in the final paragraph?* (The speed and ruthlessness of the victory.)

Extract 4

- This extract, from a non-fiction book about animals, provides information about toads. Highlight the title. Explain that it indicates what the text is about.

- Underline and read aloud the opening statement. Ask: *What does it achieve?* (It introduces and defines the subject.) Read aloud the next two sentences and discuss the first paragraph's function. Confirm that it introduces the subject of toads and answers the questions 'What?' and 'Where?

- Investigate the divisions in the remaining text (paragraphs). Underline the bold words before paragraphs two to five. Identify them as questions used as subheadings. Ask: *What is their purpose?* (The reader can access information easily.)

- Circle 'amphibian' and 'predator'. Ask: *Why are they in bold font?* Highlight the glossary to the right of the page where the words are defined. Underline 'Common Toad (Bufo bufo)' and 'Natterjack Toad (Bufo calamita)'. Explain that English and Latin names show scientific rigour in the information.

- Underline 'is found' used twice in the fifth paragraph. Identify each as a passive verb: a verb in which the person or thing receiving the action is the subject of the sentence. Circle and identify 'toad', 'Natterjack Toad' and 'Common Toad' as the subjects of these verbs.

- Discuss how the table allows us to compare the two species. Underline the two questions relating to both pictures Ask: *How is it clear which information applies to which toad?* (layout in the table)

Extract 1

As he sat on the grass and looked across the river, a dark hole in the bank opposite, just above the water's edge, caught his eye, and dreamily he fell to considering what a nice snug dwelling-place it would make for an animal with few wants and fond of a bijou riverside residence, above flood level and remote from noise and dust. As he gazed, something bright and small seemed to twinkle down in the heart of it, vanished, then twinkled once more like a tiny star. But it could hardly be a star in such an unlikely situation; and it was too glittering and small for a glow-worm. Then, as he looked, it winked at him, and so declared itself to be an eye; and a small face began gradually to grow up round it, like a frame round a picture.

A brown little face, with whiskers.

A grave round face, with the same twinkle in its eye that had first attracted his notice.

Small neat ears and thick silky hair.

It was the Water Rat!

Then the two animals stood and regarded each other cautiously.

"Hullo, Mole!" said the Water Rat.

"Hullo, Rat!" said the Mole.

"Would you like to come over?" enquired the Rat presently.

"Oh, it's all very well to *talk*," said the Mole, rather pettishly, he being new to a river and riverside life and its ways.

The Rat said nothing, but stooped and unfastened a rope and hauled on it; then lightly stepped into a little boat which the Mole had not observed. It was painted blue outside and white within, and was just the size for two animals; and the Mole's whole heart went out to it at once, even though he did not yet fully understand its uses.

Extract 2

"To my mind," observed the Chairman of the Bench of Magistrates cheerfully, "the *only* difficulty that presents itself in this otherwise very clear case is, how we can possibly make it sufficiently hot for the incorrigible rogue and hardened ruffian whom we see cowering in the dock before us. Let me see: he has been found guilty, on the clearest evidence, first, of stealing a valuable motor car; secondly, of driving to the public danger; and, thirdly, of gross impertinence to the rural police. Mr Clerk, will you tell us, please, what is the very stiffest penalty we can impose for each of these offences? Without, of course, giving the prisoner the benefit of any doubt, because there isn't any."

The Clerk scratched his nose with his pen. "Some people would consider," he observed, "that stealing the motor car was the worst offence; and so it is. But cheeking the police undoubtedly carries the severest penalty; and so it ought. Supposing you were to say twelve months for the theft, which is mild; and three years for the furious driving, which is lenient; and fifteen years for the cheek, which was pretty bad sort of cheek, judging by what we've heard from the witness-box, even if you only believe one-tenth part of what you heard, and I never believe more myself – those figures, if added together correctly, tot up to nineteen years—"

"First-rate!" said the Chairman.

"– So you had better make it a round twenty years and be on the safe side," concluded the Clerk.

"An excellent suggestion!" said the Chairman approvingly. "Prisoner! Pull yourself together and try and stand up straight. It's going to be twenty years for you this time. And mind, if you appear before us again, upon any charge whatever, we shall have to deal with you very seriously!"

Extract 3

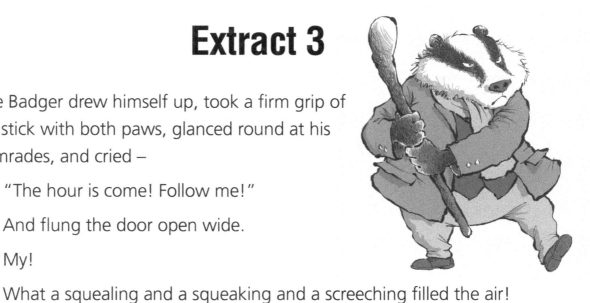

The Badger drew himself up, took a firm grip of his stick with both paws, glanced round at his comrades, and cried –

"The hour is come! Follow me!"

And flung the door open wide.

My!

What a squealing and a squeaking and a screeching filled the air!

Well might the terrified weasels dive under the tables and spring madly up at the windows! Well might the ferrets rush wildly for the fireplace and get hopelessly jammed in the chimney! Well might tables and chairs be upset, and glass and china be sent crashing on the floor, in the panic of that terrible moment when the four Heroes strode wrathfully into the room! The mighty Badger, his whiskers bristling, his great cudgel whistling through the air; Mole, black and grim, brandishing his stick and shouting his awful war-cry, "A Mole! A Mole!" Rat; desperate and determined, his belt bulging with weapons of every age and every variety; Toad, frenzied with excitement and injured pride, swollen to twice his ordinary size, leaping into the air and emitting Toad-whoops that chilled them to the marrow! "Toad he went a-pleasuring!" he yelled. "I'll pleasure 'em!" and he went straight for the Chief Weasel. They were but four in all, but to the panic-stricken weasels the hall seemed full of monstrous animals, grey, black, brown and yellow, whooping and flourishing enormous cudgels; and they broke and fled with squeals of terror and dismay, this way and that, through the windows, up the chimney, anywhere to get out of reach of those terrible sticks.

The affair was soon over. Up and down, the whole length of the hall, strode the four Friends, whacking with their sticks at every head that showed itself; and in five minutes the room was cleared.

Extract 4

Facts about toads

A toad is a small **amphibian**. There are many species of toads. Particular toads are native to different parts of the world.

What is the difference between toads and frogs?

Toads usually have dry skin with warts on it. Their hind legs are shorter and they do not hop.

Do toads prefer land or water?

A toad spends most of its time living on land, but needs water for the breeding season.

What do toads eat?

A toad is a **predator**. It usually eats insects and small animals such as worms, slugs and snails. The prey is seized by the toad's long, sticky tongue, which can extend up to 25mm.

Which species of toad live in Britain?

Two species of toad are native to Britain: the Common Toad (Bufo bufo) and the Natterjack Toad (Bufo calamita). The Natterjack Toad is found frequently in East Anglia. The Common Toad is found throughout Britain.

Glossary

amphibian: an animal that lives both on land and in water, but returns to water to lay its eggs

predator: an animal that hunts for food

	Common Toad	Natterjack Toad
How does it move?	It has a lumbering walk or crawl.	The Natterjack Toad runs or crawls on short, stocky legs.
Where is it found?	The Common Toad favours a damp area with ample cover. It is found close to water for breeding.	It is found in coastal sand dunes and is close to water when breeding.

GRAMMAR, PUNCTUATION & SPELLING ▶

---

1. Avoiding errors

Objective
To ensure correct subject and verb agreement when using singular and plural; to proofread for errors.

What you need
Copies of *The Wind in the Willows*, photocopiable page 22 'Avoiding errors'.

What to do
- Complete this activity after reading Chapter 4.

- Scan Chapter 4 together. Comment on the large number of characters and their different ways of speaking. Suggest that Grahame uses the dialogue to distinguish between their status, age and education.

- Investigate the hedgehogs' language. Direct the children to the paragraph beginning 'Yes, please sir' and the hedgehogs' subsequent speech. Ask pairs to list mistakes. Share results, identifying 'me and Billy' instead of the correct 'Billy and I' and the use of a pronoun with a proper noun in 'Billy he…' and 'Mr Badger he's…' Point out 'we was'. Ask: *What should it be? Why?* ('we were' because subject and verb should both be plural)

- Refer to the hedgehogs' departure, their respectful gestures and Rat's gift. Suggest that they need to thank him in writing.

- Give the children photocopiable page 22, 'Avoiding errors'. Present the page as a letter, written by the older hedgehog. Suggest that he has had little education and, as with his speech, is prone to errors. The children must circle the errors and then rewrite the letter in their books, correcting the errors: spelling, punctuation and lack of subject and verb agreement.

Differentiation
Support: Give the children the sheet with the errors already marked and ask them to rewrite it correctly.

---

2. Linking ideas

Objective
To link ideas across paragraphs.

What you need
Copies of *The Wind in the Willows*.

What to do
- Complete this activity after reading Chapter 5.

- Read aloud the paragraph 'He gave them sixpence…' in Chapter 4 and the first sentence of the next paragraph. Invite the children to cover 'Presently'. Ask: *What difference would omission make? Is the word needed?* Let partners discuss its meaning ('soon') and its function here. Ask: *What is its word class?* (an adverbial: a word or phrase adding meaning to the verb) Confirm that adverbials often form a smooth link between events and ideas in two paragraphs.

- Explain that adverbials are usually of two types: time or place. Time adverbials indicate when something happens (for example, 'the next day'); place adverbials indicate where (for example, 'nearby'). Ask: *Which adverbial group does 'presently' belong to?* (time)

- Identify further adverbials linking paragraphs: 'After luncheon', 'When' and 'As' in Chapter 4 (time); 'On reaching the town' in Chapter 2 and 'Once beyond the village' in Chapter 5 (place).

- Write these adverbials on the board for the children to sort into time and place: 'afterwards', 'underneath', 'the next week', 'before noon', 'on top', 'tomorrow', 'alongside', 'beneath', 'beforehand', 'around', 'along'. They must use three of them to begin and to link written paragraphs about the characters.

Differentiation
Support: Provide three short paragraphs for the children to add opening sentences to.

3. Setting aside

Objective
To use brackets, dashes or commas to indicate parenthesis.

What you need
Copies of *The Wind in the Willows*, photocopiable page 23 'Setting aside'.

What to do
- Complete this activity after reading Chapter 11.

- Comment that a word or phrase can be added as an aside to a complete sentence to give extra information or comment. This is known as parenthesis. Explain that three forms of punctuation indicate parenthesis: brackets, a pair of dashes or a pair of commas. Show these on the board. Suggest that their use can depend on author preference, but there are subtle distinctions: brackets separate an important comment; dashes interrupt with relevant information; commas supply extra information. Identify Rat's words in Chapter 11: 'and the place in such a mess (I'm told) it's not fit to be seen!' Ask: *What important information does '(I'm told)' provide? Has Rat visited the Hall since the capture?*

- Add your own examples on the board: 'Mr Toad (he was famously rich) had a new hobby'; 'Boat racing – difficult for even experts – was his new fad'; 'His new boat, bought at great cost, was very powerful'. Emphasise that the words in parenthesis are within the sentence.

- Give out copies of photocopiable page 23, 'Setting aside'. Explain that the children must identify words in parenthesis inside each sentence and add punctuation. The last four require them to add their own words, as well as adding puntuation.

Differentiation
Support: Let children work in pairs and reduce their number of sentences.

Extension: Ask children to explain to a partner why they have chosen the punctuation they have used.

4. Keeping in time

Objective
To ensure the consistent and correct use of tense throughout a piece of writing.

What you need
Copies of *The Wind in the Willows*.

What to do
- After finishing the book, comment that Toad sometimes makes mistakes with verbs. Point out his muddle with 'teach' and 'learn' towards the end of Chapter 11, and his mistakes with form and tense when he is talking to Mole earlier in Chapter 11 ('I done it'.)

- Revise what 'tense' means. Explain that it is the time in which the writing is expressed: past, present or future. Refer the children to the book's first page. Ask: *What tense has Grahame written this story in?* (past) Ask the children to tell a partner three verbs on the first page that confirm this answer. Write 'had been working', 'was moving', 'flung' and 'scraped' on the board and point out their variety.

- Set a scenario: Rat is telling Mole about Toad. Write the following on the board and ask the children to copy and complete the sentences with verbs and phrases in an appropriate tense:

- "Oh, the dreadful things Toad _____ done in the past! One year, he _____. Another year, he _____. Even last summer, he _____. He says now that he _____ a changed animal. Well, we _____ see. Only the future _____ us. If Toad does break his word, then we_____."

- Invite children to read out their sentences. Does the class think the verb tenses make sense?

Differentiation
Support: Advise that children say their sentences aloud to a partner. Also provide children with possible words to choose from to fill the gaps.

Extension: Ask the children to write what Mole says in reply.

5. Hyphens

Objective

To use hyphens to avoid ambiguity.

What you need

Copies of *The Wind in the Willows*, photocopiable page 24 'Hyphens', dictionaries.

What to do

- After completing the book, draw a hyphen on the board for the children to name the punctuation mark. Ask: *What is its purpose?* (It joins words to link meaning and to avoid confusion.)

- Comment that a hyphen can be used to link a prefix to a word. Write these pairs on the board and explain that each word in the pair has a different meaning: 're-cover', 'recover'; 'repress', 're-press'. Ask children to use dictionaries to check meanings and then place each in one of these sentences: 'The washerwoman will _____ the gown.' ('re-press' meaning to iron again); 'Toad had to _____ his excitement.' ('repress' – to keep down); 'Badger can _____ from his tiredness.' ('recover'); 'Mole promised to _____ the damaged armchair.' ('re-cover' – to put a new cover on). Share answers.

- Explain that the inclusion or omission of a hyphen between two words can also change the overall meaning. Write 'weasel-bashing Toad' for the children to read aloud. Ask: *What is Toad doing?* (Toad is bashing a weasel.) Write 'weasel bashing Toad', without a hyphen. Ask: *Who is bashing whom now?* (A weasel is bashing Toad.)

- Give out photocopiable page 24, 'Hyphens' for the children to complete.

Differentiation

Support: Encourage partner collaboration and provide support with distinguishing between the labels on the photocopiable sheet.

Extension: Ask children to illustrate 'boat-sinking Mole' with and without the hyphen.

6. Sticking together

Objective

To use a range of devices to build cohesion.

What you need

Copies of *The Wind in the Willows*.

What to do

- Complete this activity after reading Chapter 12.

- Comment that stories need cohesion and explain that this means sticking together or linking.

- List cohesive devices: determiners and pronouns referring to earlier words; conjunctions and adverbs, making relations between words clear; ellipsis of expected words.

- Identify cohesive devices in paragraphs 3 and 5 of Chapter 12: 'the' (determiner, referring back to a particular hole); 'he' (referring to Toad); 'Then' (adverb, referring back to time).

- Write this passage on the board:

  '"Stop buying vehicles, Toad!" lectured Badger. "They cost too much. You have a pile of money, but the pile will get smaller. Eventually, it could be nothing."

  Meanwhile, Toad slumped in a chair with a dreamy look on his face; that look meant he was scheming. When his plans were ready, he tried them on Badger.

  "Could I buy a bus?" asked Toad.

  "No!" replied Badger.

  "Could I buy a train?"

  "No!"

  "…an aeroplane?"'

- Ask the children to name and explain eight or more cohesive devices. Organise small groups to compare results before having a class discussion.

Differentiation

Support: Let partners work on the text before comparing answers with another pair.

Extension: Ask children to write a similar text, perhaps a conversation between Rat and Toad.

Avoiding errors

- This letter from the hedgehogs is full of mistakes. Circle the errors on the sheet and then rewrite the letter in your book, correcting the errors.

Dear Mr Rat,

It was terrible good of you to give us mony. it were a hole 6 pense each. We is very greatful and my Mum she say to rite this letter.

Me and Billy we never had so much mony before. We was so exited? We went strait too the sweet shop and bort toffy that we chewd all day do you like toffy

I were very prowd to meat your friend Mr Mole you and he is fine gentlymen. Billy and me is terrible proud to no you, sir. Will we sea you again!

We send best respex to you and Mr Mole.

Yours sincere,

Bobby and Billy Hedgehog

Setting aside

- Identify the words in parenthesis and separate them from the main sentence with a pair of brackets, commas or dashes.

1. Badger he was famously brave lived in the Wild Wood.

2. The Wild Wood very appropriately named was a fearsome place.

3. The rabbits certainly large in number were a mixed lot.

4. Sometimes the foxes even the friendly ones played frightening tricks.

5. Badger's house it was built years ago was right among them.

6. His big stick carved from the strongest oak kept him safe.

- Now add and punctuate your own words in parenthesis.

7. Mole _____

_____ longed to visit Badger.

8. His chance came when Ratty _____

_____ fell asleep.

9. The journey _____

_____ began well.

10. As it grew dark _____

_____ everything changed.

Hyphens

● Draw lines to match each label to the correct picture.

| sandwich eating Toad | sandwich-eating Toad |

● Explain how and why the labels are different.

_____

_____

_____

● Put the hyphen in the correct place in 'snaky tree roots' to label the pictures below.

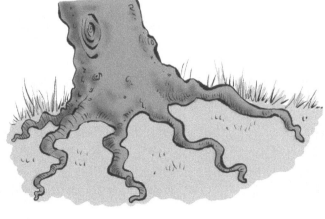

| snaky tree roots | snaky tree roots |

● Check Chapter 1 and tick the label for the roots imentioned in the story.

PLOT, CHARACTER & SETTING ▶

1. Setting off

Objectives
To predict what might happen from details stated and implied.

What you need
Copies of *The Wind in the Willows*, photocopiable page 29 'Setting off'.

What to do
- Use this activity after reading Chapter 1.

- Remind the children that a story has three strands: setting, character and plot. Explain that setting includes time and place. Point out the mention of spring, seasonal changes and the state of the countryside and river bank in Chapter 1. Read aloud descriptions of the scenery on Mole and Rat's boating trip and the chapter's final sentence. Ask: *What does Mole hear?* (wind whispering through the reeds) Ask: *Does setting seem important in this book? What places could Mole explore?*

- Ask: *Who do you think is the main character here? Why?* Agree that the chapter begins and ends with Mole's actions. Comment on 'emancipated' in the final paragraph. Ask: *What does it mean?* (freed) *What does it suggest? Is Mole going to stay on the river?*

- Discuss the plot. Ask: *Has much happened?* Share ideas, identifying Mole's exploration, discovery of a river and friendship with Rat. Ask: *Are there other animals for Mole to befriend?*

- Give out photocopiable page 29 'Setting off'. Ask the children to record their observations and predictions drawn from Chapter 1, dividing them into setting, characters and plot.

Differentiation
Extension: Ask children to justify their ideas with references to the text.

2. Ducks' Ditty

Objective
To prepare poems and plays to read aloud and to perform, showing understanding through intonation, tone and volume so that the meaning is clear to an audience.

What you need
Copies of *The Wind in the Willows*.

What to do
- After reading Chapter 2, direct the children to Rat's composition at the beginning of the chapter. Ask: *What is a ditty?* (a short, simple song)

- Read the first verse aloud. Define 'dabbling' (getting wet every so often by putting their heads into the water). Indicate the visual image 'Yellow feet a-quiver'. Ask: *What do the words show about Rat?* (his observation of the river)

- Put the children into small discussion groups to investigate the song's construction. Ask: *What do you notice about the verses? Is rhyme used? Are punctuation and repetition important?*

- Share results, indicating the separate first verse and the regularity of the following three. Identify the regular rhyme pattern, occasional exclamation marks and repetition of 'dabbling' and 'Up tails all'. Ask: *Is Rat emphasising these actions?*

- Suggest that a song is meant to be heard. Create four groups and assign each group a verse of 'Ducks' Ditty' to rehearse. The children must consider tone, speed, emphasis and volume. Encourage them to think about whether they will all perform each line or build the speakers towards the end.

- Let each group perform in order, and ask listeners to consider how the words affect their attitude to the ducks and river life.

3. Exploring characters

Objective
To draw inferences, such as inferring characters' feelings, thoughts and motives from their actions, and to justify inferences with evidence.

What you need
Copies of *The Wind in the Willows*, photocopiable page 30 'Exploring characters'.

Cross-curricular link
PSHE

What to do
- After reading Chapter 4, suggest that four important characters have been introduced: Mole, Rat, Badger and Toad. Comment on their strong friendship bonds but very different characteristics.

- Ask: *What is evident about Mole in the early chapters?* Identify willingness to explore; self-belief as he assumes control of the boat in Chapter 1; inexperience; and courage going to the Wild Wood alone.

- Investigate how Rat is presented in Chapter 1. Point out his hospitality to a new friend and kindness as he teaches Mole water skills. Ask: *What is revealed about Rat in Chapter 2? Why does he agree to the excursion in the caravan?* (He does not want to disappoint friends.)

- Ask pairs to investigate Toad and Badger's behaviour in Chapters 1 to 4. Ask: *Why does Toad leave the work to the others in Chapter 2? Is Badger pleased to hear the doorbell in Chapter 4?*

- Give out copies of photocopiable page 30, 'Exploring characters'. Explain that the children must re-read the text involved and choose two characteristics shown by each animal. They must then explain why they have chosen these characteristics and back their choices up with evidence.

Differentiation
Support: Give the children definitions of the characteristics.

Extension: Ask children to think of a third characteristic shown by each animal.

4. Reading enjoyment

Objective
To read books that are structured in different ways.

What you need
Copies of *The Wind in the Willows*.

What to do
- Complete this activity after finishing the book.

- Remind the children that books are structured in different ways. Describe another book with a different structure that the children may be familiar with, for example *Wonder* by R J Palacio: it is in the first person; is divided at irregular points into parts; narrators change.

- Use partner and then class discussion to investigate *The Wind in the Willows*. Ask: *Is it narrated in the first or third person? How is it divided up? Are divisions regular? Are there appealing headings? Is the story chronological?* Share results, identifying the third-person narration, chapters of regular lengths, chapter titles, separate incidents and story interruptions.

- Ask the children to write three ways in which they think the structure has contributed to their enjoyment of the book, and three aspects which worked less well for them. Share ideas. Invite them to consider how they would structure this book. Ask: *Would you have different divisions? Would you ever use first-person narration? Would you relate Toad's adventure in adjacent chapters?*

- Direct the children to the Contents page of *The Wind in the Willows*. Invite them to make a rough draft of their new structure, with their divisions and titles. Notes underneath should list what changes they have made. Let children present their proposals to one another.

Differentiation
Support: Encourage them to work with a partner and expect fewer original ideas.

Extension: Expect greater originality. Let them use a computer for a final, typed version.

5. True friends

Objective
To identify and discuss themes and conventions in a wide range of writing.

What you need
Copies of *The Wind in the Willows*, photocopiable page 31 'True friends'.

Cross-curricular link
PSHE

What to do

- Use this activity after finishing the book.

- Comment that the book emphasises friendship between the four main characters: Mole, Rat, Badger and Toad. Ask: *In what ways can friendship be expressed?* Encourage partner discussion before sharing ideas. Agree on four main ways: accepting differences; working together; looking after one another; loyalty.

- Direct the children to Chapter 2 where Mole, tempted by Toad's exciting ideas, promises to stick to Rat 'loyally'. Indicate the first page of Chapter 3 and Rat's reluctance to call on Badger. Ask: *What is the reason?* (Badger would not like it because he is 'very shy'.) *How is Rat showing friendship?* (He is accepting that Badger is different from him.)

- Give out individual copies of photocopiable page 31 'True friends'. Point out that the page is divided into four boxes, with a chapter and incident named in each box. Explain that the incidents identified all reveal important aspects of the animals' friendship.

- Ask the children to write notes on the photocopiable sheet before bringing the class together to discuss their ideas.

Differentiation

Support: Suggest that partners locate and discuss the incidents together before writing independently.

Extension: Ask the children to identify other incidents that show the friendship between the four animals.

6. Time's language

Objective
To discuss and evaluate how authors use language, including figurative language, considering the impact on the reader.

What you need
Copies of *The Wind in the Willows*.

What to do

- After finishing the book, suggest that the time of year is an important theme. Ask: *How?* Agree that nature's seasonal changes affect the animals' behaviour.

- Examine the opening page. Ask: *What time of year is it?* Point out 'spring-cleaning' in the first sentence, and 'sunshine' and 'soft breezes' in the second paragraph. Ask: *How is Mole affected?* (It has inspired him to go out exploring.)

- On the board, model dividing a page into three columns: the time of year; nature's changes; the effect on an animal. Write Chapter 1 on the left-hand side, and an entry in each column. Use quotation marks for the phrase quoted in the second column. Let children choose their quotation.

- Put the children into pairs to discuss Chapter 2. Ask: *What time of year is it? How are nature and animals affected?* Share some answers: 'summer' in the first line; 'golden afternoon' and 'thick orchards' on the caravan trip; ducks dabbling; Toad's exuberance. Ask the children to enter answers for Chapter 2.

- Ask pairs to investigate Chapters 3, 5 and 6 in the same way. Encourage rough notes, before making final choices for the second and third columns.

- Discuss results in groups and as a class. Ask: *Which season do you think is described most powerfully? How?*

Differentiation

Support: Indicate helpful pages for nature descriptions.

Extension: Ask children to investigate the second half of the book.

7. Understanding meanings

Objective

To check that the book makes sense to them, discussing their understanding and exploring the meaning of words in context; to draw inferences.

What you need

Copies of *The Wind in the Willows*.

Cross-curricular link

PSHE

What to do

- After finishing the book, comment that its dialogue, by animals and humans, reveals the speakers' attitudes to one another and their relative social status.

- Indicate Rat and the hedgehogs' conversation in Chapter 4. Ask: *What does the hedgehogs' poor grammar and vocabulary reveal?* (They are less educated.) *What do 'sir' and 'gentlemen' show? Do they feel equal to Rat and Mole?* Ask the children to write a paragraph about the different social standing revealed in this exchange.

- Direct the children to Chapter 8. Indicate the girl's sympathy and Toad's arrogant boastfulness. Identify dialogue where she talks about her aunt and his reply: 'There, there…' Ask: *What does he mean? Should the girl be ashamed that her aunt is a washerwoman?* Ask the children to write a paragraph about the 'social gulf' that Toad perceives between himself and the gaoler's daughter.

- Progress to Chapter 10. Divide the class in half to read the barge woman and Toad's argument aloud, from 'You common…' to '…will *not* have'. Point out 'your betters' and 'will *not* be laughed at by a bargewoman!" Ask: *Does Toad feel superior? What does the barge woman think of Toad?* Ask the children to write a paragraph about what they understand from this conversation.

Differentiation

Support: Invite partners to share their thoughts before writing a sentence or two.

Extension: Expect more writing and better understanding of important words.

8. Building characters

Objective

To draw inferences and to justify inferences with evidence.

What you need

Copies of *The Wind in the Willows*.

Cross-curricular link

PSHE

What to do

- Complete this activity after finishing the book.

- Point out that the book opens with Mole's name, and features him in most chapters after that. Explain that Grahame builds Mole's character gradually. Ask the children to sketch a timeline on a landscape piece of paper representing Mole's development through the book. They should mark points on the timeline where, later, they will write brief descriptions of his personality. Ask them to write these five headings: Chapter 1, Chapters 3–4, Chapter 5, Chapter 9, Chapters 11–12.

- Scan Chapter 1 with the children. Ask: *What sort of character is Mole at this stage? How confident is he?* Point out his ignorance (he overturns the boat) and his willingness to apologise. Ask the children to write a few sentences describing Mole at this stage.

- Repeat the activity with a combined investigation of Chapters 3 and 4. Comment on Mole's courage that fades when problems occur, his dependence on Rat, his willingness to let Rat lead. Again, children write a few sentences describing Mole's character at this stage.

- Ask pairs to make three similar investigations: Chapter 5, Chapter 9 and the combined Chapters 11 and 12.

- As a class, discuss the changes seen in Mole. Ask: *How much has Mole changed by the end?*

Differentiation

Support: Omit one or two of the stops and expect less writing.

Extension: Expect closer reference to the text.

Setting off

- Think about Chapter 1 and complete each section below.

What I have learned so far

Setting	Characters	Plot

How I predict the book will progress

Setting	Characters	Plot

The strongest clue to the author's plans:

Exploring characters

- Find and read about each incident.
- Name or choose two characteristics shown in each incident.

selfishness	pride	courage	hospitality
foolishness	bravery	impulsiveness	ingratitude
ignorance	concern	generosity	good-humour

Chapter 1

Mole capsizes the boat.

Mole shows [　　　　　] and [　　　　　].

Chapter 2

Toad is escorted safely home.

Toad shows [　　　　　] and [　　　　　].

Chapter 3

Rat goes in search of Mole.

Rat shows [　　　　　] and [　　　　　].

Chapter 4

Badger gives Mole a tour of his house.

Toad shows [　　　　　] and [　　　　　].

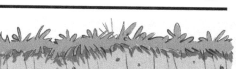

True friends

● Find and reread each incident. Then write notes on how, why and which aspects of friendship are shown in each case.

In Chapter 2, Rat agrees to join Mole and Toad on a caravan trip.	In Chapter 5, Rat visits Mole's old home enthusiastically.
In Chapter 9, Mole finds Rat in a dazed state.	In Chapter 12, the friends defeat the weasels and stoats.

TALK ABOUT IT ▶

1. Such a story!

> **Objective**
> To give well-structured narratives for different purposes.
>
> **What you need**
> Copies of *The Wind in the Willows*, photocopiable page 35 'Such a story!'
>
> **Cross-curricular link**
> Drama

What to do

- After reading Chapter 2, suggest that the caravan trip makes a strong impression on the three characters.

- Guide the children in scanning the chapter. Ask: *What are Mole and Rat's first reactions to the caravan?* (Mole is excited; Rat is dismissive of a 'fad'.) Point out Toad's exuberance as they travel the road, Rat's patience, and Mole's concern to please. Identify early morning chores done by Rat and Mole: attending to the horse, lighting a fire, fetching food. Ask: *What is Toad doing?* (sleeping)

- Investigate the accident and subsequent events. Ask: *Who organises matters? How do they all get home?* Identify Toad's 'spellbound' state and Rat's happiness on return.

- Propose that each animal tell his story of the caravan trip to fellow river-bankers. The stories need to be convincing, as they will differ. Ask the children to decide which animal to be.

- Give out photocopiable page 35 'Such a story!' Explain that the children must describe what happened to their character and how they felt. Emphasise that they will be telling, not reading, their story and that it will be in the first person.

- Suggest practising their storytelling on partners, then larger groups.

2. Think carefully!

> **Objective**
> To consider and evaluate different viewpoints.
>
> **What you need**
> Copies of *The Wind in the Willows*.
>
> **Cross-curricular link**
> PSHE

What to do

- After reading Chapter 3, express surprise that Mole enters the Wild Wood. Identify Rat's caution about the wood in Chapters 1 and 3 and the instruction about Badger. Ask: *Why does Mole ignore him?*

- Suggest that Mole is often impulsive. Identify examples, such as seizing the sculls and causing a boating accident and now this trip in Chapter 3. Ask: *Would more thinking produce better decisions?*

- Divide the class into two groups: group A represents Mole's cautious side, group B represents his impetuous side. Group A must think of comments to persuade Mole to wait; group B must think of comments to urge him to go into the Wild Wood.

- Organise the two groups into parallel lines facing each other. As Mole, walk down the 'alley' between the lines. On reaching children, nod to them to speak their comments. At the end of the alley, make your decision.

- Choose children to act as Mole and repeat the conscience alley. Does every Mole reach the same decision?

> **Differentiation**
>
> **Support:** Let partners collaborate on comments for the conscience alley.
>
> ---
>
> **Extension:** Let children create a conscience alley situation for Toad.

3. Genuine or fraud?

Objective
To participate in discussions and debates.

What you need
Copies of *The Wind in the Willows*, photocopiable page 36 'Genuine or fraud?'

Cross-curricular link
Citizenship

What to do
- Complete this activity after reading Chapter 6.

- Suggest that Toad is considerable trouble to his friends. How? (They worry about his safety and reputation and try to protect him.) Ask: *Is he ungrateful?* (He schemes, lies and runs away.)

- Refer to Chapter 2. Ask: *What unpleasant characteristics are obvious in Toad's treatment of Mole and Rat?* Identify laziness on the caravan trip; deviousness in his talk of wanting to 'give pleasure to you fellows' when he proposes the outing; gloating in getting his own way. Identify 'the now triumphant Toad'.

- Invite pairs to find evidence that Toad is a sincere friend. Share ideas, identifying hospitality to Mole and Rat in Chapter 2; Rat and Otter's compliments and description of him as 'a good fellow' in Chapter 1.

- Ask the children to decide if Toad is a genuine friend or a fraud. (Ensure that both sides are supported.) Give out photocopiable page 36 'Genuine or fraud?' The children must choose the statements they think help their case and write three new arguments supporting their view. Chair a debate, listening to arguments from both sides and from everyone.

- Encourage the children to listen carefully to your summing-up as they reach a final decision and vote.

Differentiation
Support: Encourage partner discussion. Accept one or two new arguments.

Extension: Ask children to make a different argument: why Toad should change.

4. Memorable moments

Objective
To use spoken language to develop understanding through speculating, hypothesising, imagining and exploring ideas.

What you need
Copies of The Wind in the Willows, cue cards from photocopiable page 37 'Memorable moments'.

Cross-curricular link
Drama

What to do
- Use this activity after finishing the book. Comment that there are many memorable scenes that could easily be illustrated. Invite suggestions. Share partner and then class ideas. Talk about Mole capsizing the boat in Chapter 1; the caravan road accident in Chapter 2; and Toad's escape as a washerwoman in Chapter 8. Ask: What would these illustrations reveal? Suggest that characters' facial expressions and body language show their thoughts and feelings.

- Divide the class into four groups: Mole, Rat, Badger and Toad. Give out individual copies of photocopiable page 37 'Memorable moments'. Ask the children to refer to the book, scan the four scenes, investigate their character's actions and feelings and then write notes in each box.

- Afterwards, allocate everyone a secret scene number (1,2,3 or 4). Ask them to pose as their character in their scene. Put the children in small groups to take turns presenting their 'statue'. Can the others identify the story moment? Are thoughts and feelings obvious?

- Select individual characters to pose and reveal their thoughts to the class. Ask: *Which expressions and body language revealed what characters were thinking?*

Differentiation
Extension: Ask children to identify other memorable moments and plan how to portray them.

5. Meeting characters

Objective

To participate in role play; to infer characters' feelings, thoughts and motives.

What you need

Copies of *The Wind in the Willows*.

What to do

- After finishing the book, comment that Badger often speaks and behaves strangely. Point out Badger's grumpy 'H'm! Company' in Chapter 1; his 'gruff and suspicious voice' in Chapter 4 and instruction that he is not to be disturbed. Ask: *Does Badger really believe that Mole has 'managed excellently' in Chapter 11? Is Badger trying to make Toad jealous?* Suggest that it would be helpful to question Badger directly.

- Put the children into pairs to agree on and write two questions they would like to ask him. Then organise the children into groups of four to compare questions and agree on two group questions.

- Explain the term 'hot-seat' (role play in which a character is interviewed). Put yourself in the hot-seat as Badger. Turn away and try to make a change to your appearance (add a black-and-white striped hat, for example). Turn and face the class, and invite the groups to ask you their questions, making sure that you answer in role.

- Let groups discuss what they found out about Badger's feelings and personality. Compare findings as a class.

- Select a different character: Mole, Rat or the Otter. Repeat the task as a group activity, one group member taking the hot-seat to answer the others' questions.

Differentiation

Support: Provide some question starters.

Extension: Encourage close references to the text and more perceptive observations.

6. In or out?

Objective

To use spoken language to develop understanding through speculating, hypothesising, imagining and exploring ideas.

What you need

Copies of *The Wind in the Willows*.

What to do

- Complete this activity after finishing the book.

- Comment that Otter makes frequent appearances in the book. Point out his early appearance in Chapter 1, the references to him in Chapter 7 and his role as a disguised chimney sweep in Chapter 11. Nevertheless, he is not part of the main group of friends.

- Set a hypothetical scenario: Otter wants to join the friendship group. He decides to speak to each member in turn, make his request, and find out whom he gets on with best.

- Put the children into pairs, one acting as Otter and one as Rat. Ask them to talk to each other to see how well they get on. On your signal, let partners improvise dialogue for one to two minutes.

- Stop the improvisations, but leave one pair in character for others to listen to and question about their feelings towards each other.

- Invite the pairs to repeat the exercise with a conversation between Otter and Mole, with partners exchanging the role of Otter. Leave a new pair in role for others to listen to and question. Finally, hold improvised dialogues between Otter and Badger and Otter and Toad, the children listening to and questioning one pair.

- Discuss the results. Ask: *Which animal did Otter get on best with? Will he be allowed to join the group?*

Differentiation

Support: Suggest useful conversation openers.

Extension: Expect distinctive dialogue and more searching questions.

Such a story!

● Write notes to complete the sections below and use them to help you tell the story.

Introducing yourself

Who are you? _____

How did you first feel about the caravan?

_____

_____

_____

Setting off

Did you enjoy the first day on the road?

Was it a leisurely time?

_____

_____

_____

_____

_____

The accident

What went wrong? How did you react?

_____

_____

_____

_____

_____

Going home

Was the return journey easy to arrange?

How did you feel that night?

_____

_____

_____

_____

_____

The next day

What are you thinking and feeling now?

_____

_____

_____

_____

_____

Genuine or fraud?

- Decide if Toad is really a sincere friend and tick your view.

   Toad is a genuine friend and is worth keeping. ☐

   Toad is a fraud, not a true friend. ☐

- Tick arguments that can support your view.

☐ Toad delights in being visited.

☐ Toad doesn't listen to his friends' advice.

☐ Toad lets his friends do all the hard work.

☐ Toad is a very generous host.

☐ Toad is very jolly and enthusiastic.

☐ Toad is boastful and sees himself as better than everyone else.

☐ Toad tricks his friends and sneaks out of Toad Hall.

☐ Toad says his motto in life is 'Live for others!'

☐ Toad refuses to help Rat and Mole after the caravan crash.

- Write three new arguments to support your view.

1. _____

_____

_____

2. _____

_____

_____

3. _____

_____

_____

Memorable moments

- Check the story moments for your animal.

- Make notes about what your animal's thoughts and body language.

I am _____

	My body language	My facial expression	My thoughts
1. Chapter 6 Toad shouts and kicks. Rat sits on him; Mole pulls off his driving clothes. Badger gives orders.			
2. Chapter 6 Rat and Mole pull the kicking and struggling Toad upstairs. Badger stands watching.			
3. Chapter 12 Rat, Mole, Badger and Toad creep through along the secret passage. Badger leads.			
4. Chapter 12 Badger, Toad, Rat and Mole fight the ferrets and weasels.			

GET WRITING ▶

1. Talkative Otter

> **Objective**
> To précis longer passages.
>
> **What you need**
> Copies of *The Wind in the Willows.*

What to do

- Do this activity after reading Chapter 4.

- Comment that Otter is not a main character, but is often an important source of information with a surprising amount to say. Point out his news about river activity in Chapter 1 and his explanation for his appearance at Badger's house in Chapter 4.

- Suggest that the editor asks the author to shorten Chapter 4. Grahame identifies Otter's speech beginning 'Thought I should…', which is about 475 words long, as suitable for précis. Explain that a précis is a shorter version of a passage; it includes essential information, perhaps in different words, and omits unnecessary details.

- Examine Otter's speech. Ask: *What important information does it provide?* Identify concern on the river bank about Mole and Rat's disappearance; Otter's decision to visit Badger; Otter's journey through the Wild Wood; the news from a rabbit that Mole is lost in the Wild Wood. Ask: *Which details seem unnecessary?* Identify details about the robin and geese and exactly what Otter said and did to the rabbit.

- Ask the children to reduce Otter's speech to no more than 325 words. Suggest they make notes on what to include, before using a computer to type, check word count, edit and print a final version.

> **Differentiation**
> **Support:** Let partners work together on a draft version before writing independently.
> _____
> **Extension:** Expect children to recognise the need to retain Otter's voice.

2. Toad's song

> **Objective**
> To perform their own compositions.
>
> **What you need**
> Copies of *The Wind in the Willows*, photocopiable page 41 'Toad's song'.

What to do

- Do this activity after reading Chapter 10.

- Ask: *What goes wrong for Toad at the end of this chapter?* (He runs 'straight into the river'.) *What fault does he admit to?* (being conceited) Point out Toad's promise to himself not to 'sing another conceited song'.

- Direct the children to Toad's song in Chapter 10 and read it aloud together. Point out the extra verse later in the chapter. Ask: *Who are all the verses about?* (Toad) *What do they always emphasise?* (Toad's cleverness) Identify the rhyme pattern at the ends of the second and fourth lines, and the regular verse length.

- Suggest that when Toad has recovered he will sing another conceited song about this adventure, but with a more flattering ending than him struggling in the river. Ask: *What will the content be?* Share ideas.

- Give out photocopiable page 41 'Toad's song' for the children to complete. Ask them to do a rough draft first, encouraging them to read their phrases, lines and verses aloud, either to themselves or a partner, as they work on the song.

- Afterwards, invite them to perform their compositions to one another.

> **Differentiation**
> **Support:** Suggest children limit their song to two verses.
> _____
> **Extension:** Let children work independently, without the constraints of the words on the photocopiable sheet.

3. Choose me

Objective

To identify the audience for and purpose of the writing, selecting the appropriate form and using other similar writing as models for their own.

What you need

Copies of *The Wind in the Willows*, photocopiable page 42 'Choose me'.

What to do

- Do this activity after reading Chapter 11. Encourage paired exchanges before whole-class discussion.

- Show the children two copies of the same book, but with different covers (ideally *Wind in the Willows*). Explain that when books are re-printed, new covers are often designed. Suggest that the editor of *The Wind in the Willows* wants the next publication to have a single animal on the cover.

- Ask: *Who are the four main characters of this book? Is one more important than the others?* Share ideas. Agree that Rat, Mole, Badger and Toad might all claim to be the hero of the book and deserve to be on the cover.

- Suggest that the four characters write to the editor explaining why they deserve this honour. Emphasise that each animal will have his own style, probably similar to his spoken style. Investigate the dialogue in Chapter 11 and point out characteristics: Badger's rather pompous, serious tone; Rat's fussy correctness; Mole's excited eagerness; Toad's conceited self-confidence.

- Give out photocopiable page 42 'Choose me' and ask the children to finish writing the animals' letters. Afterwards create groups so that children can read each other's requests. Hold a class vote. Which animal will be on the cover?

Differentiation

Support: Let partners collaborate on ideas before writing.

Extension: Suggest writing a request from Otter.

4. Banquet invitations

Objective

To select appropriate grammar and vocabulary, understanding how such choices can change and enhance meaning.

What you need

Copies of *The Wind in the Willows*.

What to do

- Complete this activity after finishing the book.

- Remind the children of Toad's initial horror at staying indoors and writing banquet invitations in Chapter 12. Ask: *What suddenly makes him enthusiastic?* (He sees an opportunity for boasting.)

- Point out that Toad writes the letters quickly and gives them to a weasel. Ask: *Who intercepts the letters?* (Rat) *Does Rat approve?* (He thinks they are 'simply disgraceful'.) Ask: *What is probably wrong with Toad's letters? What is their likely tone?* Share ideas. Re-read from 'A fine idea had occurred…' to 'The idea pleased him mightily…'. Agree that Toad's letters are probably boastful, exaggerate his courage and fighting skills, and brag about his adventures.

- Remind the children that early in Chapter 2, Rat describes Toad as 'simple' and 'not very clever'. Direct the children to Toad's speech in Chapter 2 beginning 'There you are!' and examine his style: frequent exclamation marks; enthusiastic vocabulary ('real life', 'excitement', 'the very finest'); grammatical carelessness (for example ''em' instead of 'them'). Suggest that these letters are likely to contain similar word selection and mistakes in his grammar.

- Ask the children to write Toad's invitation letter, perhaps to a rabbit or to Otter. Suggest doing a rough draft first before writing the final version.

Differentiation

Extension: Expect a more detailed letter that captures Toad's style.

5. Ending differently

Objective
To write narratives, describing settings, characters and atmosphere and integrating dialogue to convey character and advance the action.

What you need
Copies of *The Wind in the Willows*, photocopiable page 43 'Ending differently'.

What to do

- Complete this activity after finishing the book.

- Use Chapter 1 to investigate the author's style. Point out detailed descriptions of nature ('brown snaky tree-roots gleamed below the surface of the quiet water'); dialogue that suits the speaker's personality and the situation (Mole's excited 'Oh my! Oh my!' at the picnic spread); atmosphere ('laid his head on his pillow in great peace and contentment'); an ongoing plot ('He learnt to swim and to row.').

- Guide the children in scanning the final few pages of Chapter 12. Comment on 'an altered Toad' and the peaceful end to the book. Ask: *Could the story end differently? Could Toad remain unreliable? Could he have one more adventure or mishap?* Let partners exchange ideas for an alternative ending before sharing some as a class.

- Give out photocopiable page 43 'Ending differently' for the children to plan their new ending. Expain that they should write a brief outline of their new ending before using the boxes to write some words and phrases they may use for the natural setting, dialogue, atmosphere and significant events.

- Let partners discuss their completed plans before, independently, writing their own ending.

Differentiation
Support: Let children create picture storyboards of their ending before writing the text.

Extension: Ask children to plan and talk about a second alternative ending.

6. Presenting facts

Objective
To use further organisational devices to structure text and to guide the reader.

What you need
Copies of *The Wind in the Willows*, copies of Extract 4 on page 18.

Cross-curricular link
Science

What to do

- After finishing the book, give out individual copies of Extract 4. Question the children about it, encouraging partners to exchange opinions before you accept class answers. Ask: *Is Extract 4 fiction or non-fiction? What organisational devices are used? Why?* Identify subheadings, bold font, pictures, a comparison chart and a glossary to guide the reader.

- Comment that *The Wind in the Willows*, although fictional, also contains non-fiction elements: names of river plants, trees and wildlife; ducks' feeding habits; Toad's 'crawly' movement, described by the barge woman in Chapter 10. Refer the children to Extract 4 and the word 'crawls'.

- Comment that Grahame gives Badger pronounced characteristics. Ask: *What are they?* Confirm that he dislikes 'Society' and being disturbed; he needs considerable sleep and time alone; he is strong and fierce. Suggest discovering if the fictional Badger's characteristics belong to real-life badgers.

- Put the children into pairs or small groups to share the task of writing notes, in their own words, about a badger's animal classification, habitat, food, appearance and special characteristics. Provide research books and recommend websites.

- Ask groups to then work together to plan their page's content and layout, perhaps using computers for their finished page.

Differentiation
Support: Encourage close collaboration with other children.

Toad's song

- Complete Toad's song and then read your new lines aloud to your partner.

Poop-poop! Poop-poop! Off he raced.

Toad drove like the king of the road.

_____

_____

_____

Poop-poop! Poop-poop! On he went.

Toad steered over the grass freshly mowed.

_____

_____

_____

Poop-poop! Poop-poop! Water ahead!

_____

_____

_____

No river could stop clever Toad!

_____

_____

_____

Choose me

- In your book, write each animal's letter persuading the editor to put him on the front cover. You may use the starting sentences below if you like.

Dear Editor,

A book is a serious business. I have done some writing myself, so…

_____

_____

_____

_____

_____

Yours faithfully

Rat.

Dear Editor,

I would just love to do it! I am always keen to try new things and…

_____

_____

_____

_____

_____

Yours faithfully

mole

Dear Editor,

I am not a great one for society, but I will do my duty. My friends…

_____

_____

_____

_____

_____

Yours faithfully

Badger

Dear Editor,

Hooray! What fun! Just right for a clever Toad! The other fellows…

_____

_____

_____

_____

_____

Yours faithfully

Toad

Ending differently

- Outline your suggested new ending.

_____

- Note down words and phrases you might use, remembering to write in Grahame's style.

The natural setting

Dialogue

Atmosphere

Significant events

ASSESSMENT ▶

1. Closing the gap

Objective
To note and develop initial ideas, drawing on reading and research where necessary.

What you need
Copies of *The Wind in the Willows*, photocopiable page 47 'Closing the gap'.

What to do
- Use this activity after reading Chapter 6.

- Point out that the author sometimes leaves gaps between paragraphs. Look together at the gap between the paragraph ending 'reckless of what might come to him' and the one beginning 'To my mind'. Ask: *What does this space suggest?* (Time has passed.)

- Read aloud the final sentence of the paragraph before the gap and the first two sentences of the paragraph after the gap. Ask: *What does Toad do during the time lapse?* Point out the Chairman's list: stealing a car, driving dangerously and cheeking a policeman. *How does Toad change between the two passages?* Indicate the Chairman's description of Toad's 'cowering' manner and the instruction in a later paragraph to 'Pull yourself together and try and stand up straight'; contrast this with the image of Toad who 'chanted as he flew' in the first paragraph.

- Suggest that it would be interesting to know the details of what happens, who is involved and why Toad's mood changes. Comment that Grahame may have initially planned these details.

- Ask the children to produce Grahame's possible plan for this missing part. Give out individual copies of photocopiable page 47 'Closing the gap' for the children to complete. Keep the plans for the next activity.

Differentiation
Support: Encourage brief notes and some use of drawings.

2. Missing pages

Objective
To describe settings, characters and atmosphere and integrate dialogue to convey character and advance the action.

What you need
Copies of *The Wind in the Willows*, the children's completed photocopiable page 47 'Closing the gap'.

What to do
- Do this activity after completing the previous activity 'Closing the gap'.

- Direct the children to the first paragraph of Chapter 6. Investigate the author's narrative style. Look at the use of semicolons: sometimes to avoid full stops and capital letters, and sometimes to make lists easier to understand. Guide the children in exploring the style of the subsequent three pages: the integration of dialogue into the story; spoken language that reflects personalities (for example Toad's spirited 'Shan't!' and Badger's serious 'Now then!'); Grahame's adherence to direct speech punctuation rules with quotation marks and separate paragraphs.

- Remind the children of the work they did in 'Closing the gap'. Look again at this gap and guide the children in scanning the events leading up to and following it. Encourage them to remind themselves of what they planned, perhaps by explaining the outline to a partner.

- Ask the children to use their notes to write the chapter's missing pages. Remind them to use the past tense and keep to Grahame's style.

Differentiation
Support: Let partners spend time explaining their notes to each other first.

Extension: Expect children to show an awareness of Grahame's style and reflect this in their writing.

3. Background noise

Objective
To check that the book makes sense to them, discuss their understanding and explore the meaning of words in context.

What you need
Copies of *The Wind in the Willows*.

Cross-curricular link
Science

What to do

- After finishing the book, comment on nature's background noise in the story.

- Point out the water sounds in Chapter 1: the river's 'gurgle', 'rustle', 'chatter' and 'babbling'; the weir's 'tumble'; a millwheel's 'dripping'. Read Chapter 1's final paragraph aloud. Ask: *What does Mole hear?* (the wind)

- Ask the children to write a short paragraph about Mole's discovery of noises on or near the river, giving at least two examples and quoting sound words. Ask: *Which noise do you think Mole is most excited by? Why?*

- Direct the children to Chapter 7 and indicate the noise of 'the wind playing in the reeds and rushes and osiers'. Later, Rat and Mole listen to 'wind playing in the trees': Mole compares it to 'far away music'; Rat hears 'dance music', 'words' and finally 'reed-talk'. Ask the children to write about the wind sounds, quoting from the text. Can they suggest why Rat hears more?

- Refer to the book's title. Ask: *What location do willow trees prefer?* (near water) Ask the children to write a short paragraph saying what they expected when they first heard the book's title. Did they link the title to a noise? What do they understand about the title and sounds after finishing the book?

Differentiation
Support: Encourage children to prepare with a partner. Help them to locate sound references.

Extension: Expect a firmer grasp of the topic and credible opinions.

4. Animal-etiquette

Objective
To identify and discuss themes and conventions across a wide range of writing.

What you need
Copies of *The Wind in the Willows*.

What to do

- Use this activity after finishing the book.

- Write 'etiquette' on the board and ask the children to explain its meaning to a partner. Share definitions and quote a dictionary one, for example: 'the usual rules of behaviour in polite society'.

- Suggest that animal-etiquette is a strong theme in this book. Can the children remember occasions when it is mentioned? After partner and class discussion, identify examples in Chapter 1: Mole apologises for being 'rude' when not listening to Rat; Mole cuts short questions about the Wild Wood animals because further questions would be 'against animal-etiquette'; Mole remembers 'animal-etiquette' when Otter disappears suddenly. Similarly, in Chapter 4, when talking about Toad to Badger, Mole and Rat remember 'the rules of animal-etiquette' regarding winter; and at the end of Chapter 5, 'tactful' Rat ensures Mole's evening is successful. Discuss these events, what is done that is polite and the behaviour that would be impolite. Suggest the children note page numbers and make brief notes on the conclusions reached in the discussions.

- Ask the children to write three or four short paragraphs, explaining what animal-etiquette means; why it is important to the animals' happiness and identifying two examples: what a character does that is polite and the impolite behaviour avoided.

Differentiation
Support: Expect shorter paragraphs and encourage preliminary partner discussion.

Extension: Ask children to write about the remaining examples.

5. A different Toad

Objective

To ask questions to improve their understanding.

What you need

Copies of *The Wind in the Willows*.

What to do

- After finishing the book, suggest that Toad is very different from other main characters.

- Write this question on the board: 'How is Toad's home different?' Let partners exchange ideas before class discussion. Indicate Chapter 2's description: 'handsome, dignified old house of mellowed red brick, with well-kept lawns reaching down to the water's edge'; and 'upstairs' in Chapter 6. Ask: *How does his home differ from Badger's, Rat's or Mole's?* Point out that they live in holes underground or in the river bank; his house sounds like a human's.

- Write this on the board for partner and then class discussion: 'How is Toad's conversation different?' Comment that he talks to people in Chapters 6, 8 and 10. Ask: *Does the reader hear conversations between human beings and Mole, Rat or Badger?* (They rarely speak to humans.)

- Write on the board: 'How is the plot different for Toad?' After partner and class discussion, identify Toad's involvement with a wider world (roads, cars, gaol, train and canal) and comical situations (he dresses as a washerwoman).

- Ask the children to copy the three questions, writing a short paragraph in answer to each with references to the text. Finally, they should copy this question: 'Is Toad too different?' before writing whether his differences improve or spoil the book for them.

Differentiation

Support: Let children omit one of the first three questions.

Extension: Expect interesting points and apt textual references.

6. Book review

Objective

To assess the effectiveness of their own and others' writing.

What you need

Copies of *The Wind in the Willows*.

What to do

- Complete this activity after finishing the book.

- Suggest that you have not studied this novel with this school year for some time. Explain that you are interested to know what the children thought of the book.

- Use paired and then class discussion to exchange opinions. Ask them to consider the book's length, level of difficulty, plot, characters and setting. Ask: *Did the book keep your attention? Did talking animals seem 'real' enough to you? Was the plot interesting? Did you enjoy the focus on rural scenery? Would you recommend it to your age group? What did you most enjoy about the book? Which aspect was least successful?* Encourage children to justify their views with references to the text. Emphasise that there are no correct answers: everyone can have a different opinion or reaction to the book.

- Invite the children to write a review of the book. Explain that a review has no set format, but is usually not too long, includes the title and author, a brief outline of the plot (without revealing too much), a personal opinion, and a comment on its suitability for others.

- Suggest the children make notes and do a rough draft before writing their polished review.

Differentiation

Support: Give children three or four specific questions to answer fully before they begin writing (for example: What happened in the book? Did you like reading it?) Encourage them to use their answers when writing their review.

Extension: Expect more enlightening reviews with original comments.

Closing the gap

● Write the planning notes for the missing part of Chapter 6.

This is what happened…

…to the car	**…to Toad**

…to the people involved	**…to Toad's mood**

SCHOLASTIC
READ & RESPOND
Available in this series:

Key Stage 1

978-1407-18254-4

978-1407-16053-5

978-1407-14220-3

978-1407-15875-4

978-1407-16058-0

978-1407-14228-9

978-1407-14224-1

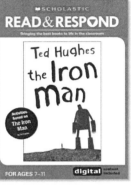
978-1407-14229-6

978-14071-6057-3

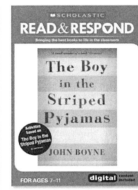
978-14071-6071-9

Key Stage 2

978-14071-6069-6

978-14071-6067-2

978-14071-4231-9

978-14071-4223-4

978-14071-6060-3

978-14071-5876-1

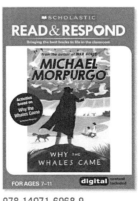
978-14071-6068-9

978-14071-6063-4

978-1407-18253-7

978-1407-18252-0

To find out more, call 0845 6039091
or visit our website www.scholastic.co.uk/readandrespond

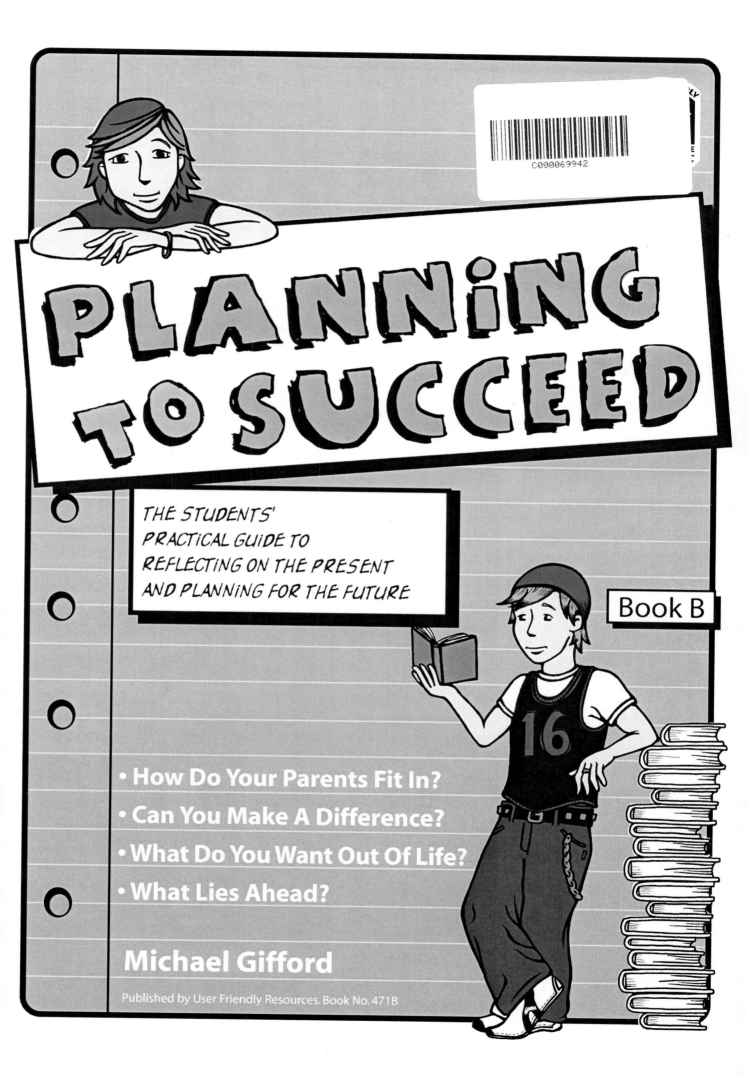

PLANNING TO SUCCEED

THE STUDENTS'
PRACTICAL GUIDE TO
REFLECTING ON THE PRESENT
AND PLANNING FOR THE FUTURE

Book B

- **How Do Your Parents Fit In?**
- **Can You Make A Difference?**
- **What Do You Want Out Of Life?**
- **What Lies Ahead?**

Michael Gifford

Published by User Friendly Resources. Book No. 471B

C000069942

TITLE

Series Name: **Planning to Succeed**

Book Name: a students' practical guide to reflecting on the present and planning for the future

Book Number: 471B

ISBN Number: 1-86968-269-6

Published: 2006

AUTHOR   Michael Gifford

ACKNOWLEDGMENTS

Designer: Anita McLeod

Editor: Pauline Scanlan

PUBLISHERS

User Friendly Resource Enterprises Ltd.

United Kingdom Office

c/- AFM Ltd.

Units 8, 9, 10, Parkside

Laughton

Shortgate Lane

East Sussex BN8 6DG

Ph: 0845-450-7502

Fax: 0845-450-7501

New Zealand Office

PO Box 1820

Christchurch

Tel: 0508-500-393

Fax: 0508-500-399

Australian Office

PO Box 914

Mascot, NSW 2020

Tel: 1800-553-890

Fax: 1800-553-891

WEBSITE

Visit our on-line shop: www.userfr.com

COPYING NOTICE

COPYRIGHT

User Friendly Resources specialises in publishing educational resources for teachers and students across a wide range of curriculum areas, at early childhood, primary and secondary levels.

If you wish to know more about our resources, or if you think your resource ideas have publishing potential, please contact us at one of the above addresses.

contents

introduction

In their last years at school many students feel de-motivated and disinclined to look towards the future. They have few ideas about what the world can offer them (or what they can offer the world!). This series provides teachers and students with a focus for honestly exploring future possibilities in positive and enabling ways.

In two write-on books, *Planning to Succeed!* contains these units:

Book A

- Who Are You?
- What's Your Attitude Like?
- Are You "Balanced"?

Book B

- How Do Your Parents Fit In?
- Can You Make A Difference?
- What Do You Want Out Of Life?
- What Lies Ahead?

Throughout, students are invited to reflect and make notes on their present lives and see how their current choices can affect what happens in the future.

These photocopiable books provide a framework that can be easily used by careers advisers, school guidance counsellors and other teachers who work alongside seniors in a pastoral capacity. Sections can be run off for students to work through independently or to discuss in small groups. The two books are packed with:

- Tips on dealing with issues that affect young people
- Motivational stories
- Activities that support critical reflection
- Planning sheets and templates

SECTION FOUR

How Do Your Parents Fit In?

I t's a hard one to get your head around – the role of parents … You're probably at that stage in your life where they irritate you and seem intent on stopping you doing things. At the same time your parents are wondering what happened to that cute and funny 10 year old they used to have. It's a dilemma found in every household in this country.

how do I manage my parents!?

Teenagers

Fed up with your stupid parents?

Then leave home, get a job and pay your own bills.

Do it now - while you know everything!

Do you think there's a daughter or son in the world who has never had an argument or confrontation with her or his parents? Doubt it! Because of the emotional bond we have with our parents, anger, distress, embarrassment, frustration, resentment, hurt, rage, guilt, and disappointment are some of the feelings we may have towards them from time to time. And if you ask your parents what negative feelings they have towards you from time to time, the same words are likely to appear!

But hopefully, their overriding emotion towards you will be one of love - whatever you do. The problem is that our egos, our 'I am right' stances, and our refusal to back down often get in the way of positive communication.

Do these typical parent statements sound familiar to you ? –

"For the 20th time, clean your room,"
"Turn down that terrible music,"
"Don't forget to take out the rubbish,"
"Stop annoying your sister," "No, you can't go out tonight,"
"Get off the telephone – no more calls tonight."

What about these responses?

"You're the pits,"
"You don't understand,"
"Everybody else's parents think so ... why do you have to be different?"
"You're the worst mother / father in the world,"
"You're not fair,"
"You pick on me."

Meaningful communication and negotiation is a two-way process. You need to engage with your parents as much as they need to engage with you.

Consider these hints for getting on with parents and others:

Hint 1: ## TRY TO UNDERSTAND THEM

Put yourself in your parents' shoes and try to see situations from their point of view. Even try to imagine that your parents are right some of the time!

The trick is to try and "walk around in their shoes" for a while and see what the world looks like. Before a brave moves from one village to another, the Sioux Indians pray: "Great Spirit, help me never to judge another until I have walked two weeks in his moccasins."

You may not like it when you are told you can't go out, that you can't have the car, or that you need to tidy up your room. But have you looked at things from your parents' point of view? Until you are able to step back and try to understand where they are coming from and the reasons for their decisions, arguments and confrontations will continue.

Two battleships had been at sea on training manoeuvres for several days in stormy weather. On one evening, with fog making visibility exceptionally difficult, one Captain remained on the bridge to guide proceedings.

Shortly after dark the lookout called down,

"Light ahead of us on the starboard bow."

"Is it steady or moving astern?" the Captain called back.

"Steady, Sir." The Captain immediately realised he was on a dangerous collision course with the other ship. He called to his signalman. "Signal that ship - We are on a collision course. Advise you to change course 20 degrees."

The signal was sent and a reply received. "Advise YOU need to change course 20 degrees."

The Captain was firm. "Send again. I'm the Captain. Change course 20 degrees."

"I'm a seaman second class," came the reply. "You had better do the changing, Captain."

By that time the Captain was furious with this insolent reply. He snapped. "Send, I'm a battleship. Change your course 20 degrees NOW."

Back came the signal, "I'm a lighthouse."

The Captain changed course! He was forced to change his view. He now saw things from the other person's point of view.

Try LISTENING first - not just hearing what is being said, but actually listening. Most problems between people occur because of poor listening, or misinterpreting what or why something is said. The way we see things is a result of our experiences, and other people's experiences might be quite different from ours. To understand others we need to be able to change the way we see things and to look at them from another point of view.

THE PARENTS' CHARTER

PARENTS   have the right to act like human beings; that is, they have the right to fall into sudden and irrational rages, to change their minds without reason, to contradict themselves, and to be stubborn, prejudiced and bloody-minded. In short, to act like their children.

PARENTS   have the right freely to hold and express opinions without being scoffed at, sneered at, or discriminated against. If they consider in all sincerity that Eminem ranks slightly behind Mozart, that is their business entirely.

PARENTS   have the right to decide on their own personal appearance. A father does not wish to be told that his hair is too short, his tie too wide, and his braces old-fashioned. Nor does he want a nose piercing for father's day.

PARENTS   have the right to freedom from unnecessary worry. If it takes you four hours to nip out for a bag of chips, it will not occur to them that halfway down the road you decided to join a protest march in town in favour of teachers' salaries. Instead they will assume you have been kidnapped, knocked down, murdered or some grisly combination of all three.

PARENTS   have the right to their sleep. If you promise to be in by 12.30 am they will not wish to be still counting the flowers on the wallpaper at 3.00 am in the morning.

PARENTS   have the right to enjoy their own homes. This becomes difficult if one of the bedrooms appears to have been converted without building permit into an indoor piggery. You may argue that your room has nothing to do with them. But a glance at the signature on the cheque that pays the bills will prove otherwise.

PARENTS   have the right to criticise and rebuke their children without fear of reprisals. In this context, 'reprisals' shall mean muttering, sulking, screaming, slamming doors, making motions with the right hand as if winding up a gramophone, and threatening to run away from home, saying "I didn't ask to be born."

PARENTS   have the right to be able to grow deaf gracefully, and in their own time. They do not need to be reminded that for a teenager, noise, cacophony, heavy metal, rap, and an unrelenting beat may be normal.

PARENTS   have the right to expect a reasonable return for their labours. Having for years acted as unpaid nursemaid, cleaner, nightwatchman, valet, banker, laundress, cook, sports coach, guidance counsellor, odd job man, and general dogsbody, they are entitled occasionally to ask you to put out the rubbish bin or mow the lawns.

PARENTS   are not to be humiliated for their own inadequacies. They may not be addressed in Japanese, expected to make head or tail of modern mathematics, or interrogated in meaningless technological jargon. At school dances they have the right to request a foxtrot without being mocked.

PARENTS   have complete freedom to nag, cajole, warn, scold, forbid, and offer unsolicited advice - not because they enjoy it, but because they have a duty to exercise their most precious and inalienable right.

Parents have a right to be parents.

SECTION FOUR: How Do Your Parents Fit In?

ACTIVITY TWENTY NINE:

Understanding Parents

Note down up to three occasions recently when you and your parents, parent, or caregiver, have had a disagreement. What was the disagreement over? How did you respond? Look at each situation from your parents' point of view. Can you understand their position?

Disagreement	My Response	My Parent(s') viewpoint
1.	....	....
....	....	....
2.	....	....
....	....	....
3.	....	....
....	....	....

Discuss your responses above with your parents. Did you correctly understand their viewpoint? Or were there other considerations you didn't know about?

Hint 2:

LOOK FOR A COMPROMISE OR BE CREATIVE

In dealing with other people, and particularly with parents, teachers and bosses, pick your battles carefully. Not all situations require the equivalent of a battalion to sort them out. Others will not be winnable at all. Some require compromise, so that all parties have some sense of satisfaction. Others again may require some lateral thinking and a creative approach before a successful outcome is reached.

It is generally good policy to look for a compromise, but first to understand exactly what each party wants, and what would be involved in this compromise.

So, compromise is important, but it needs to be a compromise that is fully understood by all.

Lateral thinking and creativity are useful tools in dealing with most situations in life. Often this will involve a challenge to, or questioning of, the 'rules.' The search for creative solutions to problems or dilemmas can be fun, too, and it is surprising what can emerge.

Two sisters squabbled, each wanting the only orange on the table. The wise parents decided on a compromise solution. The orange was cut in half and each girl given an equal portion. A sensible compromise? Yes, but .... The first sister immediately peeled her half, ate the fruit, and threw away the skin. The second sister also peeled her portion, threw the fruit away and grated the peel into the cake she was making.

The compromise was 50% successful. Had the sisters really explained their needs to each other and to their parents, the compromise would have been unnecessary, and both would have enjoyed 100% satisfaction.

ACTIVITY THIRTY:

Compromise and Creativity

Think about a home situation where compromise and creativity have achieved a positive outcome. Is there a current home situation you can use these techniques on?

....

....

....

....

....

....

....

....

....

One reason why rules need challenging or re-examining is that people can get locked into one approach or strategy for solving a situation without realising that different strategies might be more appropriate.

Roger Van Oech has written an amusing and entertaining book on creativity entitled A Whack on the Side of the Head. In this book he sets out a reason for re-looking at rules.

1. We make rules based on reason that make a lot of sense.
2. We follow these rules.
3. Time passes and things change.
4. The original reasons for the generation of these rules may no longer exist, but because the rules are still in place, we continue to follow them.

Does this sound familiar?

Creative thinking involves escaping from, and altering, out-of-date rules and replacing them with new ideas and rules.

Hint 3:

LEARN TO NEGOTIATE

In many cases, arguments with parents are over trifles that do not really matter. Remember what you looked at in Recipe for Life Book A, "don't sweat the small stuff." Be prepared to give way on issues that are of little importance. On the other hand, when you feel strongly about a situation, this will be the time to work things through with your parents. But be very clear about this - you won't "win" or get your own way all the time. So don't expect it. Be realistic, be flexible and be prepared to compromise.

Try the process of negotiation, set out on the next page.

the SIX STEP PROCESS to negotiating with your parents

PREPARE

Brainstorm a list of everything you want out of the situation. List as many wants as possible, then prioritise into **Must Have**, **Should Have**, **Could Have**. Must Have is the top priority. But remember, be realistic about your wants. See things from your parents' point of view in advance - then you'll be ready for their responses.

MEET

Find a mutually good time to discuss the situation. State your position and agree to no arguments, no raised voices. Keep to the point and don't bring up the old issues. One useful hint is that no-one can make a point until he or she has stated the other person's viewpoint satisfactorily. Put your case and question until you get at least the 'must have' wants you are requesting. If you can't get a Win-Win situation (a solution that benefits both you and your parents) it is better to disagree agreeably. It then becomes a No Deal situation. Accept your parents' decision before it degenerates into a Win-Lose situation.

PROPOSE

Use 'I' statements and be specific.
If I .... (give you, do for you, compromise over) what you want,
will you be willing to give me some of what I want?"

BARGAIN

Proposals become bargains. Agreements occur here.

AGREE

"As I understand it, I'll .... and you'll ...."
Be specific.

FOLLOW UP

Fulfil agreements.

This six step process is a guide only. Not all negotiations will follow this process.

SECTION FOUR: How Do Your Parents Fit In?

ACTIVITY THIRTY ONE:

Negotiating with Parents

Ask your parents to co-operate with you in monitoring your understanding of each other over the next week or two. If there is a discussion and potential disagreement over an issue, ensure that you, firstly, understand their point of view; and that they, secondly, understand yours. Negotiate and record the results of this process.

Issue	Negotiation and results
....	....
	....
	....
	....
	....
	....
....	....
	....
	....
	....
	....
	....
....	....
	....
	....
	....
	....
	....

Hint 4: BUiLD UP YOUR TRUST ACCOUNT

Developing and maintaining positive and trusting relationships with your parents, peers, spouse and adults, is perhaps the most crucial, and also the most difficult, of human tasks. We are surrounded by unhappiness, misunderstanding, broken relationships, bitterness and hate. All are a result of broken-down communications and a lack of trust.

If you build up a reserve of honesty, respect, kindness, courtesy, faithfulness, commitment and understanding your 'Trust Account' will be in a healthy state, even if from time to time you make mistakes and make a 'withdrawal.'

If, on the other hand, you are dishonest, thoughtless, discourteous, and show lack of respect, commitment and understanding, your Trust Account will be overdrawn and your trust level will be zero.

One problem is that we often speak or act impulsively. Words once uttered, or actions once committed, cannot be taken back.

> The advice of Mohammed is worth recalling here. When a man asked him how he might make amends for falsely accusing a friend, he was told to put a goose feather on each doorstep of the village. The next day Mohammed said, "Go and collect the feathers." The man protested. "That's impossible. The wind blew all night and the feathers are scattered beyond recall."
>
> "Exactly," said Mohammed, "and so it is with the hurtful and reckless words you spoke against your neighbour."

Far better to count to ten, wait, and hold your words or actions. You can also write a letter outlining your frustrations or anger, but wait three days before deciding whether to post it or not. Odds on, your anger will have subsided, and the situation will not seem so important several days later.

TRUST ACCOUNT

When I Keep My Word	When I Don't Keep My Word
increases	Trust
	Confidence
	Self Respect
	Self esteem decreases

There's NO right way to do the wrong thing!

So it is important that deposits into your Trust Account far exceed your withdrawals. In order to communicate and negotiate effectively you need to maintain a positive balance. Look for genuine and sincere opportunities to build up your Trust Account:

- Listen to the words, thoughts and needs of others.
- Understand - try to see things from their point of view.
- Look for win-win situations rather than win-lose arguments.
- Display courtesy, manners, thoughtfulness and kindness.
- Keep commitments, promises and confidences.
- Discuss your expectations calmly and sincerely.
- Be honest, loyal, faithful.
- Apologise sincerely when you are wrong. Do something immediately to correct the situation.
- Learn to forgive.

ACTIVITY THIRTY TWO:

Build up your Trust Account

Make a list of positive deposits you can make into your Trust Account to help improve communication and relationships with your parents and your special friends. (Be specific not general in this list).

Parents: **Deposits**

....

....

....

Friends: **Deposits**

....

....

....

ACTIVITY THIRTY THREE:

Add to your | Personality Wheel

- In the next circle of your wheel add words and thoughts that will help you cope with the stresses of life and develop your communication and negotiation skills.

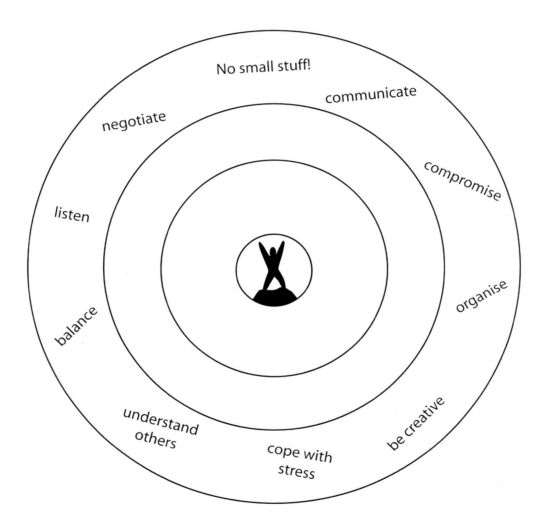

SECTION FIVE

Can You Make A Difference?

yes you can! absolutely

A man was walking on the beach when he saw in the distance a young girl coming towards him who appeared to be dancing alongthe seashore, bending from time to time, throwing her arms outand running and dancing again. When she reached him, he stopped her and said: "Hello there - I have been watching you dancing and stooping as you've come closer to me along the beach. What actually are you doing?"

"Oh," she said. "I'm picking up starfish and throwing them back into the water so they won't die in the sun."

"But there are millions of starfish on millions of beaches all over the world," said the man. "What makes you think you can make any difference?"

The girl looked at him quite severely for an instant but then picked up a starfish and hurled it back into the sea and replied, "Well, I sure made a difference to that one!"

Individuals can make a difference.

14 year old Jane made a difference. She started a project to tidy up the suburb where she lived. "I thought this area looked really grotty and I wanted to tidy it up a bit," she said. She also wanted to keep the area in which she was proud to live attractive for everyone. "I think this is a really neat place and the graffiti was giving it a bad name." So she started a project, helped by her younger brother Tim, and found support from the local business association which donated paint and rollers. The youngsters received flak from some members of the public for their efforts- some thought they were being punished for being taggers themselves - but they received much support and favourable comment. And although graffiti sometimes started to return to their freshly painted walls, this became less of a problem as they persevered with their service to the community.

Jane and Tim made a difference.

Mike Shapland made a difference.

Captain Mike Shapland of the British army is another who made a difference. He is a real hero to the children of Kuchini School in Bosnia. During his time as a United Nations peacekeeper, Captain Shapland was not just a soldier but a humanitarian. He made it his mission to search for, and provide, books and classroom materials to the youngsters in this school who had lost everything in the terrible war which had occurred in the region. By his actions, the children of Kuchini School were able to continue their education and realize that there was hope in the midst of despair.

And how many people remember New Zealander Rebecca Oaten? Very few, I suspect, but the evidence is visible every day on the difference she has made. Rebecca became known as the Helmet Lady. After tragically losing one of her own children in a cycling accident, she campaigned for six years for compulsory helmet use by cyclists. Her campaign was successfully concluded when the New Zealand parliament passed an act which made the wearing of helmets compulsory for all cyclists. I wonder how many lives have been saved through her persistence?

Rebecca Oaten certainly made a difference.

His name was Fleming, and he was a poor Scottish farmer. One day, while trying to make a living for his family, he heard a cry for help coming from a nearby bog. He dropped his tools and ran to the bog. There, mired to his waist in black muck, was a terrified boy, screaming and struggling to free himself. Farmer Fleming saved the lad from what could have been a slow and terrifying death.

The next day, a fancy carriage pulled up to the Scotsman's sparse surroundings. An elegantly dressed nobleman stepped out and introduced himself as the father of the boy Farmer Fleming had saved. "I want to repay you," said the nobleman. "You saved my son's life."

"No, I can't accept payment for what I did," the Scottish farmer replied, waving off the offer.

At that moment, the farmer's own son came to the door of the family hovel. "Is that your son?" the nobleman asked. "Yes," the farmer replied proudly.

"Then I'll make a deal with you. Let me take him and give him a good education. If the lad is anything like his father, he'll grow to be a man you can be proud of." And he did.

In time, Farmer Fleming's son graduated from St. Mary's Hospital Medical School in London, and went on to become known throughout the world as the noted Sir Alexander Fleming, the discoverer of penicillin. Years afterwards the nobleman's son was stricken with pneumonia. What saved him? Penicillin.

The name of the nobleman? Lord Randolph Churchill. His son's name? Sir Winston Churchill.

Farmer Fleming made a difference.
Randolph Churchill made a difference.
Alexander Fleming made a difference.
Winston Churchill made a difference.

Apart from the characters in the last story, none of the others is famous. They are not politicians, sports heroes, or entertainment stars. They are ordinary people, like you and me. And they have made a difference to others and to their communities.

Why not use these people as your examples, and say, "If they can make a difference, so can I." Be prepared to take a stand for something you believe in, to make a difference in your relationships, in your sports teams and clubs, at school and in the community.

This section started with a story set on a beach. Let's finish with another.

Will you make a difference in your life?

The answer is in your hands.

A young boy came up to an old man walking along the seashore. He had his hands cupped, and said, "Old man, in my hands I have a bird. Tell me whether the bird is alive or dead."

The old man looked at the boy and said quietly, "Son, if I say the bird is alive, you will crush it, open your hands and show me a dead bird. If I say the bird is dead, you'll open your hands and let the bird fly away. So I say, the answer lies in your hands."

ACTIVITY THIRTY FOUR:

Making a Difference

Through your reading of books, magazines and newspapers, make a list of people who in their lives have made a difference to others. You will find examples everywhere, almost daily, perhaps even among your own friends and family.

ACTIVITY THIRTY FIVE:

Being Remembered

Sit down and consider how you would like to be remembered. Write a list for yourself below. Include all the skills, qualities, interests, passions, responsibilities, roles, and successes you plan to achieve in your lifetime. Be specific:

I'd like to be remembered for: ....

....

....

....

....

....

....

SECTION SIX

What Do You Want Out of Life?

dreaming

You can dream. You need to dream. Dreaming is the first step towards achieving what you want from your life. And, DREAMS are FREE. So what are your dreams for this year and for the future?

If you can dream it ... You can live it

ACTIVITY THIRTY SIX:

Dreaming

Let your mind wander and dream of the things you want most out of life. Don't restrict yourself in these dreams, but ensure that what you dream, you really want. Write down this List of Dreams in the categories below.

LIST OF DREAMS

For my education: ....

For my career: ....

For my finances: ....

For my family life: ....

For where I live: ....

For my travels: ....

For people I know: ....

Other dreams:

....

....

You can make your dreams become a reality by understanding that you are the architect of your own life. You can make everything happen yourself by believing that you can.

If you sit there and wait for life to happen 'to' you ... you'll be waiting a long time. Sure ... there is the occasional lucky chance that might come your way - but these will be the exception, rather than the rule.

No-one owes you a living ... If you don't put anything into life ... it won't give you anything back. It's a simple equation, but one which many students fail to 'get'.

To get what you want - to pass an exam, to buy that car, to get that job, to win that race .... Guess what? You won't get it sitting round at home watching the telly. It WONT fall out of the sky and into your lap. To make your dreams happen you need to act on them. You begin by setting goals. Look at these three people who dreamed ... and then achieved.

Nelson, Tiger and Lydia – Three Dreamers

Nelson Mandela had a dream for a united South Africa while he was a political prisoner under the white South African regime. His dream was realised when he finally, after years of imprisonment, became President of the South African Republic, a dream reinforced at the opening of the 1995 Rugby World Cup, when the South African team, inspired by a morale-boosting pep talk from the President, defeated world champions Australia in the opening match.

Today Nelson Mandela can look back on all that he has achieved, against incredible odds.

Today Tiger Woods is the world's No. 1 golfer.

In April 1997, 21-year old Tiger Woods scored an awe-inspiring victory in the highly prestigious US Masters Open Golf Tournament. Woods had fantasised since he had first started playing golf about winning the Masters, although he did not expect his first victory would be so spectacular - winning by 12 strokes with a record score of 270.

"It's a wonderful thing to see someone live up to his dreams," said his proud father after the marvellous win.

Turning dreams into a reality means identifying and setting goals. This takes time and planning; most goals can't be reached overnight. Think of all the training Lydia Bradey had to do before she summitted Everest. Dreams are usually achieved incrementally by making small steps towards them.

In 1988 the first woman to climb to the summit of Mount Everest without bottled oxygen was New Zealander Lydia Bradey. She retraced Sir Edmund Hillary's route to the top. Bradey was 14 when her mother sent her on a mountain craft course. "I think I was terrified, but it was good. It was fantastic actually." In the year she turned 18 she climbed Mt Cook. twice. Then she set her sights on Everest … eight years later she achieved it.

Today Bradey runs a company which takes adventurers into Mongolia.

Set Some Goals

Your goals need to be:

Measurable - you need to be able to measure whether you have achieved the goal.

Attainable - the goal must be able to be accomplished.

Specific - the goal must be clear and specific.

Time Framed - you must set a time for the completion of the goal.

Extending - a goal needs to stretch and extend you.

Realistic - a goal must be realistic for you.

Use this **MASTER** technique when setting goals.

Goals need to be challenging

But still realistic

Out of reach But not out of sight

One Way To Start Off

Let's say you want to set a straightforward goal like being able to run 10 kilometres a day by the end of November. How would you go about it. First apply the Master technique.

Try to establish weekly goals for improvement (e.g. increase time spent training by one percent). The more realistic the goals are, the less likely you are to become discouraged part way. Remember, your goals can be qualitative (e.g. getting into shape) or quantitative (e.g. running 5 miles in under 50 minutes).

Establish both short and long term goals: Make daily, weekly and monthly goals.

Short term: I am going to go out and run even if the weather is terrible and I don't feel like it.

Long term: I will be able to run seven kilometres by the end of September.

Monitor your progress: Try keeping a log book to reinforce your daily step by step progress towards the achievement of the goal.

Record your goals: Commit to your goals by writing them down. Review your progress on an active basis. Have faith in yourself! Is there a dream goal you have? Perhaps to run a marathon one day?

Modify your goals: It's fine to change your goals! As you make progress, your short term and even long term goals may change. Modify your goals according to changes in circumstance and document the changes. What would happen if you pulled a muscle and couldn't train? Realise and accept you might not always be able to attain your goal.

THINGS TO THINK ABOUT

- *What long-term goal would you like to achieve? Is this goal realistic? Be honest! Explain why you think you can achieve the goal.*
- *What short term goals do you need to set to achieve the long term goal?*
- *Is there a related 'dream goal' that is years away?*
- *What obstacles might you encounter trying to meet your goal?*
- *How could you overcome these obstacles?*

ACTIVITY THIRTY SEVEN:

You be | the Adviser

Read the brief profiles of the following students and advise each on their choice of goals using the MASTER technique as your guide.

Jenny is 15:
She is shy and nervous, and does not contribute much in class because she finds academic work difficult. However, she is an exceptional diver, and competes without nerves in national diving contests.

Jenny wrote these as her goals:

- *To be a secondary school teacher (her mother's dream really).*
- *To represent Britain in diving at the 2008 Olympic Games.*

Your Comments: ....

....

....

....

Tahu is 18:
He has been top of his class in languages (French and Japanese) throughout his secondary schooling. He has learnt the piano for several years, but does not practise as he is too busy with sport and social activities. He's also the drummer in his school's award winning band.

Tahu wrote these as his goals:

- *To be tour guide in Europe by the time I am 21, and own a tour company by the time I am 27.*
- *To be based in New York and working as a drummer in a band when I have made my fortunes from travel at age 33.*

Your Comments: ....

....

....

....

....

Who has the responsibility for setting your goals?

- Your parents?
- Your teachers?
- Your friends?

All wrong. Only YOU.

Others can offer advice, but only you can set your goals.

Now let's set some goals!

A French naturalist, Jean Henri Fabre conducted an experiment, in which caterpillars were placed on the rim of a flower pot. Inside the pot were pine needles, their main source of food. But with so much food centimetres away, the caterpillars just crawled around the rim and eventually died from starvation and exhaustion. They had no goals of their own - they just followed the others.

ACTIVITY THIRTY EIGHT:

Goals for this Year

STEP ONE:

Take some or all of the areas above, and for each, write down the goals you wish to achieve, the date by which you wish to achieve them, and then in the first column, your current situation regarding each goal. Remember to use the MASTER technique (p.24) when setting each goal.

for example,

SCHOOL GOALS		
Current situation	This year's goals	Completion
Averaging 55% in Geography and English.	75% in Geography, English	November
Averaging 60% in Maths and French	85% in Maths; 80% in French	November

STEP TWO:

Consider what it is going to take to get from your current situation to the achievement of each goal. You will need to consider what extra skills and knowledge you have to acquire, what difficulties or obstacles may stand in your path and how you will tackle these, including what help or advice you might need from other people.

For example,

Self-improvement goal:
To achieve distinction in my Grade 6 clarinet performance exam.

Skills/Knowledge
Learn 5 clarinet solos.

Difficulties/Obstacles
Finding time to practise.
Fingering technique.
Memorising the solos.

Solutions/Help
Start daily practise times.
See Mr Bates for help.
Memorise bit by bit.

Action Plan:
Monday – 7.30 am: begin 30 mins daily practice before breakfast.
Tuesday – Ask Mr Bates about finger exercises at my weekly lesson.

The charts on the next four pages might be helpful.

GOAL CHART

SCHOOL

Current situation   This year's goals   Completion

SELF-IMPROVEMENT

Current situation   This year's goals   Completion

FITNESS

Current situation   This year's goals   Completion

FAMILY

Current situation   This year's goals   Completion

STICK THIS ABOVE YOUR DESK AT HOME AS A CONSTANT REMINDER

GOAL CHART

CAREER

Current situation	This year's goals	Completion

MONEY

Current situation	This year's goals	Completion

SOCIAL

Current situation	This year's goals	Completion

OTHER _____

Current situation	This year's goals	Completion

STICK THIS ABOVE YOUR DESK AT HOME AS A CONSTANT REMINDER

ACTION PLAN

SCHOOL GOALS: _____

Skills/Knowledge	Difficulties/Obstacles	Solutions/Help

Action Plan:_____

_____

SELF-IMPROVEMENT GOALS: _____

Skills/Knowledge	Difficulties/Obstacles	Solutions/Help

Action Plan:_____

_____

FITNESS GOALS: _____

Skills/Knowledge	Difficulties/Obstacles	Solutions/Help

Action Plan:_____

_____

FAMILY GOALS: _____

Skills/Knowledge	Difficulties/Obstacles	Solutions/Help

Action Plan:_____

_____

ACTION PLAN

CAREER GOALS: _____

Skills/Knowledge	Difficulties/Obstacles	Solutions/Help

Action Plan: _____

_____

MONEY GOALS: _____

Skills/Knowledge	Difficulties/Obstacles	Solutions/Help

Action Plan: _____

_____

SOCIAL GOALS: _____

Skills/Knowledge	Difficulties/Obstacles	Solutions/Help

Action Plan: _____

_____

OTHER GOALS: _____

Skills/Knowledge	Difficulties/Obstacles	Solutions/Help

Action Plan: _____

_____

ACTIVITY THIRTY NINE:

Dreams Revisited

Now look back to your Dream List (Activity 36). Examine each dream using the MASTER technique. Do you need to amend any of your dream goals?

LIST OF DREAMS

For my education: ....

For my career: ....

For my finances: ....

For my family life: ....

For where I live: ....

For my travels: ....

For people I know: ....

Other dreams:

....

....

think outside the square

I M A G I N A T I O N

"Imagination is more important than knowledge, for knowledge is limited to all we know now, and understand, while imagination embraces the entire world, and all there ever will be to know and understand"
Albert Einstein.

Being able to dream means having imagination. All the great thinkers in the world have been able to imagine, to "think outside the square", to think laterally, and to imagine things as they might be in the future. All the great inventions of civilization have been the result of thinking and experimenting outside the norm, of looking for unusual solutions to apparently insoluble problems.

Here's a good example of 'thinking outside the square.'

A primary school teacher gave her class of five-year-olds a colouring assignment. She told them, "On this sheet of paper you will find an outline of a house, trees, flowers, clouds and sky. Please colour them with the appropriate colours." One of the students, Aroha, put a lot of work into her colouring, and was disappointed when the drawing was returned to find a big black "X" on it.

She asked the teacher for an explanation. "I gave you an X because you didn't follow the instructions," the teacher said. "Grass is green, not gray. The sky should be blue, not yellow as you have coloured it. Why didn't you use the proper colours, Aroha?"

"But I did," the girl replied. "That's how it looks to me when I get up early to watch the sunrise."

The teacher had assumed there was only one correct answer. Aroha was looking at it from a different perspective.

The following activities are designed to get your imaginative juices flowing!

ACTIVITY FORTY:

Creativity Exercises

A. COTTON REELS

You have two minutes to write down as many uses as you can for a cotton reel.

B. PAPER CLIPS

Choose five items from the following list and write down the most creative uses you can find for each, using a paper clip with each item.

orange	ear	glass	tea	watch	potato
chair	tree	window	kitchen	garden	house
leaf	pigeon	wine	Germany	table	bottle
newspaper	maid	radio	shoe	wood	book
lightbulb	pub	water	handbag	cup	pepper
holiday	banana	pen	could	dinner	mirror

C. BRICKS

Imagine that you are a consultant for a brickyard that makes common red construction bricks. The brickyard is in financial difficulties. The manager of the brickyard is interested in new uses for his products and has asked you to provide him with some. Spend three or four minutes in pairs thinking about the problem, and then write down some new uses for bricks.

Hint: To improve your creativity, make a list of the attributes of a brick and then make your list. These could include - roughness, weight, colour, strength, shape etc.

E. THE IRRITATIONS LIST

Take a pencil and paper and construct a list of irritations in your life. If you run out of bugs before 10 minutes, you are either suffering from some sort of block, or have life unusually under control!

Let your Irritations List spark ideas in your mind for inventive solutions. The list should ensure that specific areas of need are illuminated and that you have put in a reasonable amount of flexibility of thought. Choose two or three irritations with potential for new inventions. What solutions have you? Can you design new plans?

D. THE LIFE GAME

Take a real situation (which can often be lifted straight out of the headlines) such as a strike, a leak of dangerous chemicals, a natural disaster. Give yourself a specific role (e.g. CEO of a company, Prime Minister, union leader) and work out a possible solution to the problem from your point of view. Try playing the game with others so that you can respond to their thoughts and solutions. Develop the skills of communication, or justifying, planning and persuading, looking at consequences, sharing ideas etc.

Sample Irritations List:

TV dinners	Blunt pencils	
Plastic flowers	Burnt out light bulbs	
Buying a car	Noisy clocks	
Relatives	Newspaper ink that rubs off	Red tape
Paperless toilets	Small, yapping dogs	Corks that break in the bottle
Rotten oranges	Soft ice cream	Chlorine in pools
Cleaning the oven	Prize shows in TV	Writing letters
Broken shoe laces	Throw-away cans	Locating books in libraries
Cloudy ice cubes	One sock	Smelly exhausts
Removerless price stickers	Cigarette smoke	Cold tea
Dripping taps	Wobbly chairs and tables	Blunt knives
Pictures hanging on an angle	Big bunches of keys	Thorns on rose bushes

F. WHAT IF?

Asking 'What if' questions is a powerful way to get the imagination going. You simply ask 'what if' and then finish the question with an unusual or even impossible idea or situation. Then answer your question creatively.

Another way to stretch the imagination is to ask 'What if' someone else was solving your problem. How would - for example -

> **Examples**
> - What if men also had babies?
> - What if we only lived to 22 years old?
> - What if people didn't need to sleep?
> - What if we were born with a third eye in the back of our heads?
> - What if everyone in the world spoke only Japanese?

your school principal, Queen Victoria, Mother Teresa, Mahatma Ghandi, Harry Potter, Nelson Mandela, Kylie Minogue, your grandad go about it? What special expertise would they bring? What different perspectives would they add? What might their solution be?

Cort Thinking

In his books on lateral thinking, the writer Edward de Bono encourages people to use a variety of strategies to solve problems and expand the mind. Some of these include:

PMI (Plus Minus Interest)

In this strategy, you take a topic and list all the Plus, Minus and Interesting factors (those which are neither Plus nor Minus) involved in thinking about or discussing that topic.

CAF (Consider All Factors)

In this strategy, you think especially of those factors which most people would not consider as part of their thinking. A friend bought a new car recently, and tried the CAF strategy. He looked at colour, seats, engine capacity, fuel consumption, comfort, and so on. But when he drove the car home, he realised he had not considered all factors! His new car did not fit into his garage!

Six Hats Thinking

In this De Bono strategy, you "put on" different hats in order to see all sides of a situation or problem.

Red Hat Thinking involves feelings, hunches and intuition. There is no need to justify feelings or emotions. They just are!

White Hat Thinking involves being neutral. There are no opinions or interpretations, just facts, figures, information, data.

Yellow Hat Thinking represents the advantages. The benefits, the values, the opportunities, and the reasons why something will work.

Green Hat Thinking is the creative hat. This covers proposals, suggestions, alternatives. It gives scope for lateral thinking and creativity.

Black Hat Thinking is negative, the devil's advocate. The emphasis is on why something can't work, why it can't be done, why it is a bad idea.

Blue Hat Thinking is an overview of a situation, rather like the conductor of an orchestra - an ability to see all sides, and to come to a conclusion.

ACTIVITY FORTY ONE:

PMI and CAF   Exercises

Do a PMI on one or more of these topics:

- Schools should operate from 7.00 am to 1.00 pm for six days a week.
- Cars should be manufactured with a top speed of 50 kph.
- All children should learn the violin.

Do a CAF on one or more of these topics:

- Going on a family holiday.
- Moving to a new town.
- Changing careers.
- Asking someone out
- Not handing in an assignment

ACTIVITY FORTY TWO:

Wearing The Six Hats

In a group of six, with each student "wearing a different hat", discuss the following topics.

- Money is the root of all evil.
- Teachers should be paid according to their results.
- There should be no age restriction on the purchase or consumption of alcohol.

As in all things in life, there is a balance between your dreams and reality, but if you do not have dreams, and set out of reach (for the moment) goals you will not realise your hopes or achieve them. Aim for the best you can possibly do. Now let's begin.

STEP THREE:

Begin.
"What? Now?" you may ask.
Yes, NOW.

"How do you start a journey of 1,000 miles?
(answer: take the first step).

"How do you eat an elephant?"
(answer: one bite at a time).

"How do you begin any task?"
(answer: take the first step, and then one bit at a time).

One good way of getting started NOW, and taking the first step, is to write out your goals for each week, prioritise them, and see yourself achieving them.

get your priorities in order

A. Each week make a list of what you aim to accomplish in the following seven days.
B. Give each item a priority rating A, B or C.
C. As the week progresses, go through the list and complete each item in order of priority.
D. When each item is completed tick it off and feel your accomplishment.

You can also break down your Weekly Priority Plan into A Daily Plan. This will give you a daily focus on what must be done.

Looking ahead, you can prepare a Monthly Priority Plan, which will enable you to sort out your aims on a more long-term basis. As the year progresses, items in the 'can wait' column will move across to the 'do soon' column and eventually be included in the 'do now' list.

> *Achieving today's goals* will act as a foundation for *this week's goals*.
>
> *Achieving this week's* goals will provide stepping stones for *this month's goals*.
>
> *Achieving this month's* goals will be a major impetus towards succeeding in *this year's goals*.

Catch-up Time

It is important to build some "catch-up" time into any study programme or goal-achieving programme. There will be occasions when your timetable is interrupted for very good reasons, and there will also be times when you don't finish a task in the time available.

So, keep a couple of hours aside over each weekend for any catch-up tasks. And towards the end of each month keep another few hours free for catch-up use if you need them.

Just knowing that these times are available will reduce your stress and enable you to complete tasks properly, rather than rush through them or leave them unfinished.

Your aim will be to start each new month with a clean slate! No jobs outstanding, no tasks incomplete, no worries, and the next month's plan ready to be implemented.

The Big "P" ...

Ah yes ...and then there's the Big 'P'. ...

Two words need to be eliminated from our vocabularies - 'SHOULD' and 'TRY'. How often do we hear comments like, 'I should get started on this assignment,' or 'I'll try to do some saxophone practice today'? Either you will get started and you will do your practice or you won't. By using 'should' and 'try' you are really only setting up your excuse for when you don't do these activities. "I tried to do my sax practice, but there were too many other things on my plate!"

We all indulge in our pet time-wasters, and need to be aware of these if we are to avoid using them as excuses for not beginning or accomplishing a task.

What do you think The Big P is?

ACTIVITY FORTY THREE:

My Pet Time Wasters

List your pet time-wasters here. By noting them down, you will not fool yourself so easily when you find yourself indulging in them!

....

....

....

....

In The Success Workbook (Gifford, 2000, User Friendly Resources), fifteen Procrastination-Busting Techniques are listed (yes the Big P means 'procrastination'). These are summarised below, but you may wish to read about them in more detail in that book.

1. Do it NOW!
2. The Salami technique – break tasks into smaller, manageable segments.
3. Do the hardest, most difficult task first.
4. Do anything associated with the task to get you going.
5. Give yourself five minutes to work on some aspect of the task.
6. Promise yourself a reward when you have completed the set task.
7. List the positive things that will occur as a result of finishing the task.
8. Ask a friend, teacher or parent to help you get started.
9. Begin the task at the time of day when you are at your best.
10. Establish a set time and routine for starting your tasks.
11. Use procrastination-busting affirmations and display these on your wall..."I will use no more excuses!"
12. Use a mentor who can help to keep you on task and be your sounding board.
13. Brainstorm a topic or task for five minutes.
14. Keep the difficulties and frustrations of a task in perspective.
15. Remember previous occasions when you have tackled a difficult task successfully.

SECTION SIX: What Do You Want Out Of Life?

ACTIVITY FORTY FOUR:

Overcoming Time Wasting

Discuss techniques for overcoming time-wasting and note down the ones that seem to be most effective for you. Keep this list handy or pin it on your wall, so that when you feel moved to waste time, instead of getting on, make a decision on which technique will get ACTION and the task you're avoiding underway.

1. ....
2. ....
3. ....
4. ....
5. ....
6. ....
7. ....

a year planner

Many organizations now display large Year Planners on the walls of offices. On these all the important dates, meetings, seminars, conventions, presentations and so on are listed, and added to as the year progresses.

ACTIVITY FORTY FIVE:

My Year Planner

It is very helpful to have an overview of your year. Get a Year Planner from your careers' office or local bank, and start blocking in major items such as holidays, exam weeks, sports tournaments, camps and school productions. Then add regular weekly and monthly activities, completion dates for assignments, special events and reminders. By using different colours for different items, you will see instantly where you are at, how you are progressing, and what time you have left for your specific weekly goals.

These three slogans might help you as you work through your year!

"Don't Sweat The Small Stuff"

We all need reminders to keep things in perspective and not to waste time letting small things take over, Dr. Richard Carlson writes, "I've never met anyone (including myself) who hasn't turned little things into great big emergencies. We take our own goals so seriously that we forget to have fun along the way ... Or we beat ourselves up if we can't meet our self-created deadlines. Most people create their own emergencies, and life does go on even when things don't go according to plan."

"The Main Thing Is To Keep The Main Thing The Main Thing"

At different times in the year, some activities energies or tasks will take precedence over others. At the time of a school production, for example, The Main Thing for those involved will be rehearsals and performances. Later in the year, the examinations must take priority. At any given time then, The Main Thing is to keep The Main Thing The Main Thing.

"Each Step Leads Me Closer To My Goal"

This one speaks for itself.
No-one ever got anywhere by standing still.

review your goals

From time to time goals need reviewing. In the light of experience you may wish to alter some of your goals, or replace them with others. There is nothing wrong in this. In fact, it shows strength to be able to evaluate how far you have come, and if the goals you originally set are the right ones for you. If they are no longer relevant to you, or if they are out of sight AND out of reach, it is time for a change.

It doesn't matter how far you have gone towards a goal, if your ladder is leaning against the wrong wall, every step you take just gets you to the wrong place faster!

Maria left school with the goal of being a lawyer. For a year she worked in a solicitor's office and took university exams leading to a law degree. But she began to realise that I didn't want to be a lawyer at all!! She wanted to be a mountain guide. Her ladder was leaning against the wrong wall, and she had to decide whether to go all the way to the top of the wrong wall, or accept that the 'law goal' was a mistake. She's now grateful that she was able to change her career goal, obtain the support of her parents and friends in the process, and enjoy a lifetime in the outdoors scaling some of the world's highest peaks.

ACTIVITY FORTY SIX:

| A Goal | Achievement Review

Use the chart following to review your goals for the year. Six months is often a useful time for a review. You have an opportunity to amend your goal or its completion date, or you may need to find extra resources, time or obtain help from others ('The Future'). Photocopy this chart to give you further opportunities for review.

GOAL ACHIEVEMENT REVIEW

Goal: _____

Review date: _____

Progress: _____

_____

Concerns: _____

_____

The Future: _____

_____

_____

Goal: _____

Review date: _____

Progress: _____

_____

Concerns: _____

_____

The Future: _____

_____

_____

Goal: _____

Review date: _____

Progress: _____

_____

Concerns: _____

_____

The Future: _____

_____

_____

life's road is often crooked

So you've dreamed your dream, you've set your goals and you're working assiduously to achieve them. It won't be easy, which often makes achieving what you want that much sweeter.

Life will always throw obstacles in your path. Think about ways to hurdle over these obstacles. See them as learning curves rather than blockades. Here are just a few:

- Family problems
- Alcohol and drugs
- Competition
- Health issues
- Peer pressure
- Poverty
- Rejection
- Despair

Sometimes it might seem as though everything and everyone is against you. But know this, - things will ALWAYS improve. Even though it never seems like it at the time ... and you want to throw in the towel or curl up into a ball. It will never stay as bad as this. There is always someone you can turn to to talk about your obstacles: a friend, parent, school counsellor or someone else you trust. Believe it.

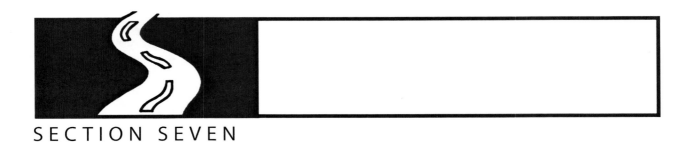

SECTION SEVEN

What Lies Ahead?

preparing for the future

Your final years at school provide an excellent opportunity to carry out your own personal preparations for life after school. There are plenty of experts both within your school (such as careers advisers, guidance counsellors, and individual teachers) and in the local community who will be able to advise and assist you as you build up your knowledge and resources.

Among the areas you will need to consider are:

Writing A Curriculum Vitae (CV)

Curriculum Vitae is a Latin term meaning Course of Life. A CV is an essential as you look for casual, temporary or permanent employment. The presentation of this document will tell a prospective employer about your school achievements, your experience, your personal skills and attributes, and also about you as a person.

There are various ways of compiling a CV, and you will need to look at which format suits your personality and style. Most will probably include the following:

Personal details - full name, address, other contact details, schools attended, qualifications are the most basic details people provide. Some people add in things like "birth date and place", "health status" and "marital status" - but you need only put the personal details you feel comfortable revealing. There's no law against the bare minimum of details here.

A photograph is usually included in a CV nowadays.
- School awards and responsibilities.
- Employment record (starting with the most recent).
- Skills, abilities and interests.
- General information - statement of your aims, goals, beliefs.
- Names of two or three referees. Make sure you ask their permission first, before including them on your CV.

A CV needs to be updated from time to time, to include your most recent qualifications, work experience, and other relevant information.

ACTIVITY FORTY SEVEN:

Preparing your CV

Prepare and write your CV after looking at different models and obtaining advice from teachers and your family. Look on-line for models too. A well-presented CV can mean the difference between getting an interview for a job or not.

Budgeting

Most students in their last years at school have begun to save (and spend!) money earned through evening or weekend work. Learning to manage this money requires careful budgeting - especially if you have a goal in mind like driving lessons, a holiday away with your friends, or even books for a new tertiary course. Credit cards, chequebooks, hire purchase agreements and loans all include the seeds of disaster unless you learn how to use them to your advantage.

It is important to stay in the 'black' while you build up your finances. In particular, be wary of the high interest charged on credit card repayments. These can be crippling for the unwary. And look for ways to save money. A well-cooked, balanced meal can cost half what a (probably) less nutritious takeaway meal will cost. Take a shopping list to the supermarket, and keep to it. This will keep you on track and help you from picking up too many extras and specials which you don't need.

The key to successful budgeting is to know your limits and stick to them. Don't be afraid to ask for advice.

ACTIVITY FORTY EIGHT:

Preparing a Budget

A. Imagine you are a first year student at a university. You have a part-time job, and you still live at home. Note down your average monthly income, and then consider your monthly expenses. These could include: transport costs (car or public transport), clothing, food (when not eating at home), board to your family, course expenses (fees, field trips, stationery etc), gifts, insurances, social or sports club expenses, social activities, repayments, medical and dental expenses, mobile phone expenses, general expenses. Can you balance your budget? Be realistic.

B. Imagine yourself as a second year student. You have a part-time job, but you now share a flat. What additional expenses might you be faced with? These could include rent, food, power, telephone, extra furniture and household equipment, newspapers. Can you balance your budget? Have you anything left for savings or investment?

Research

You will need to consult parents and specialists in order to obtain appropriate advice in areas such as medical and personal insurance, investments, saving and superannuation, vehicle costs, mortgages and loans, health and fitness issues, legal matters, and employment contracts.

ACTIVITY FORTY NINE:

My Personal Budget File

Make a list of areas in which you need advice, the names and details of the contacts you make, and the decisions you make in each of these areas. In some cases, these will involve expenditure which you will need to consider when finalising your budget.
For example:

Area	Contacts	Decisions
Medical Insurance	'X' Company Janet Goodson Ph: 437 0614 jgoods@hotmail.com	Basic medical insurance £20 per month. Starting 1 February.

Applying For A Job

Applying for a job is like most things of value in life - the more effort you put into it, the more likely you are to succeed. There are many different tactics and approaches you can use when starting a job search, depending on whether you are looking for a part-time job to help pay expenses while studying, or a permanent job as a start to your career path. In the first instance, the type of job may not necessarily be important, but in the second, you need to have your sights fixed on the future, and how you plan to get there. The activities on skills, qualities and behaviours in the first sections of this workbook (Book A) will help you clarify your aims and goals, as well as highlight your personal attributes.

How Do You Find A Job?

- Research has shown that using the Internet to check websites for jobs, and posting CVs to possible employers have little chance of success.

- Answering advertisements in newspapers or magazines can be more successful. At least you know there is a job available, but you may be one of fifty or a hundred applicants, and so have to take your chance in this competitive world. This problem is also recognised by employers, who often will not advertise a vacancy as they do not wish to be inundated with applications. These employers prefer to employ new staff recommended to them by someone they know.

- Some people have success by approaching private employment agencies. These agencies will have a number of prospective employers on their books, and this will increase the likelihood of your success.

- One effective way of looking for a job is to ask parents, friends, teachers and other contacts if they can help with leads. A personal recommendation is a very positive way of obtaining a job. You can't expect to be head-hunted early in your career, but once you are known in the workforce, it is surprising how often new opportunities arise. There may be an opening in the firm or company your mother works in, or a friend may know of someone looking for a person with your expertise.

- Visit possible firms or offices in which you could have an interest and ask whether any vacancies are likely to occur in the near future. Try to arrange for a short interview with the manager or personnel manager. Use the Yellow Pages to identify firms or organisations which interest you, and telephone to make an appointment to see the appropriate person to discuss employment prospects. Leave your CV with them (include a photo so that they can remember who you are!)

Remember … employers won't come knocking on your door!

When applying for a job in writing, the first essential thing is to present a well-written covering letter. It needs to be brief, clear, and make the prospective employer sit up and take notice. You would like him or her to say, "Now this is a person I would like to meet."

Many employers will immediately reject applications addressed to "Dear Sir / Madam." They will expect you to have taken the trouble to find out the name of the person who may be employing you. Similarly they are likely to reject you if you spell their name, or the name of their organisation, incorrectly, or if your application contains spelling mistakes. Using a spell-check on the computer is NOT infallible. You need to check spelling personally, using a dictionary if in any doubt.

It is sometimes helpful to say that you will follow up this letter after a few days by making a personal telephone call. Provided you then keep to your word, it will show an employer that you are serious about the application.

ACTIVITY FIFTY:

Writing a Job Application Letter

Write a reply to the following advertisement placed in the local newspaper.

WANTED:

A bright young student to begin permanent work in our city megastore. The successful applicant will have a cheerful personality and a keen interest in books, music and the entertainment industry.
Apply in writing to Jonathan Welbrow, Personnel Manager, Virgin Books, 1233 Queen Street, London.

Ask your parents or a family friend involved in business to check your letter and comment on it.

Job Interviews

When you secure an interview for a job, the first rule is to be prepared. Do some homework on the organisation. Find out how it operates, the names of people you are likely to meet in the interview, and if possible speak to people who already work there.

Go to the interview with a set of questions you would like answered, because an interview is a two-way process. You need to know whether the job is right for you, just as the employer needs to gauge whether you are the person to fill the vacancy.

Rehearse your questions and answers in advance. Visualise yourself in the interview situation, meeting your prospective employers, relaxing during the interview, and acquitting yourself well.

Dress appropriately. What you wear will vary according to the type of job you are applying for. But whatever you wear, ensure that your clothes are clean, and that you present the best possible image of yourself.

When shaking hands, offer a firm grip, not a wet fish dangling hand, or a bone cruncher. During the interview, look at people in the eye, speak clearly, and be yourself. Address people by name if you can remember them. Avoid nervous mannerisms. Smile to relieve the tension. It is normal to be nervous, but the interviewers could be just as nervous as you are!

Typical questions you may be asked at an interview include:
- Tell us a little about yourself.
- What do you know about our organisation?
- Why are you applying for this position?
- What are your greatest strengths?
- What are your main weaknesses? (A trick question! Good responses to this kind of question are things like ... "I probably expect too much of myself and others," or " My tendency to work through lunch breaks"!) The point is to make a positive sound like a weakness.
- Why do you think you may be suitable for this position?
- What has been your greatest success at school or in your life / work?
- What has been your greatest disappointment?
- What are your main interests and hobbies?
- Where do you see yourself five years from now?
- What people do you admire most?

Answer questions honestly and sincerely.

People often talk themselves out of a job, by going on and on during the interview. So restrict your answers to between 30 seconds and 2 minutes for any one question. Talk about yourself only when it seems relevant.

As you leave, thank them sincerely for talking with you.

Depending on the circumstances, many people write a thank-you note to the organisation afterwards, addressed personally to the main interviewer.

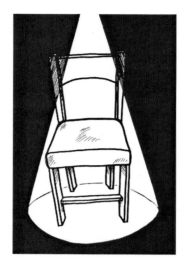

ACTIVITY FIFTY ONE:

A Mock Interview

Ask a parent or teacher to run through a mock interview with you, and obtain feedback on your appearance, mannerisms, clarity of speech, answers to questions and the questions you would like to put to the organisation yourself.

Expectations of Employers

Most employers today expect their staff to have gained some academic or skill-based qualification. For some it may be a national school qualification, for others it will be evidence of successful tertiary study.

The interesting thing is that, apart from specific job-related qualifications - such as a Veterinary Science degree for a vet; or a travel qualification for working in the travel industry - most employers want to know that you have had the application, commitment and determination necessary to get a qualification, but the actual qualification is not necessarily important.

Read the extracts from letters sent by two companies to prospective employees.

We seek women and men with a Bachelor of Applied Science degree, majoring in rural valuation and farm management. In addition we seek: strong interpersonal skills, good planning and organisational skills, computer skills, a driver's licence, the ability to accept responsibility for a high value portfolio, the ability to learn new skills, and a strong service commitment.

(Here, a specific academic qualification is required, but the remainder of the qualifications mentioned are personal skills and abilities).

> Our employees need to be able to communicate well, and to relate to groups of clients, as well as to individuals. They need to be genuinely interested in people, non-judgmental, sensitive and outgoing. A sense of humour is also helpful. In some cases we have to lead our clients down a new path, and in doing this, they need to be encouraged and motivated to change what they may hold as a firm goal, objective or belief.

(In this example, no specific academic qualifications are needed. Here, a prospective employee will be judged on his or her personal strengths).

In other words it is your qualities, skills and behaviours, as discussed in Sections 1, 2 and 3 that employers are looking for. The need for tolerance, understanding and seeing the other person's point of view will also be important qualities in most jobs. Check back on these sections before tackling Activity 52 below.

ACTIVITY FIFTY TWO:

What Will my Employers Expect of Me?

Imagine that you are the Manager of a Travel Company with ten branches throughout the country. You are looking for a Public Relations consultant, whose job it will be to work with staff in promoting the Company as a good place to work, and encouraging clients to make their travel bookings through the Company.

What skills, attributes and behaviours will you be looking for in prospective employees?

....

....

....

Discuss your requirements with others and see what similarities and differences there are in your lists.

ACTIVITY FIFTY THREE:

A Visit to Employers

Take the time to visit employers in a variety of industries or companies in which you may have an interest in working at some time. Ask them for their requirements when taking on new staff.

REFLECTIONS

- What would you like to do, have, or accomplish this year?

  _____

- What would you like to do better?

  _____

- What do you wish you had more time for?

  _____

- What would you like to have more money for?

  _____

- What are your unfulfilled ambitions?

  _____

- What would you like to get others to do?

  _____

- What barriers or blocks exist in your life?

  _____

- In what ways would you like to be more efficient?

  _____

- If you could teach everybody in the world just one thing
  - an idea, a skill, a fact, a value - what would it be?

  _____

- If you had just 30 days to live what would you do differently? What is
  stopping you from doing some of these things now?

  _____

- What would you like to accomplish in your life?

  _____

YOUR PLAN TO SUCCEED

Now that you've worked through the activities in *Planning to Succeed* - what would you say are the key ingredients that will lead towards your life being happy and successful?

_____

_____

_____

_____

_____

_____

_____

_____

_____

_____

_____

_____

_____

_____

_____

_____

_____

References

- Bolles, R (2002) What Color is Your Parachute? Ten Speed Press, Berkeley.

- Buzan, T (1988) Make the Most of Your Mind, Pan, London.

- Carlson, R (1997) Don't Sweat the Small Stuff, Bantam, Milsom's Point.

- Covey, S (1989) The Seven Habits of Highly Successful People, Simon and Schuster, New York.

- De Bono, E (1999) Lateral Thinking, Penguin, London.

- De Bono, E (1999) Six Hats Thinking, Penguin, London.

- Gawain, S (1995) Creative Visualisation, Nataraj Publishing, Novato.

- Kehoe, J. (1987) Mindpower, Zoetic, Toronto.

- Schwartz, D (1984) The Magic of Thinking Big, Thorsons, Wellingborough.

- Selye, H. (1978) The Stress of Life, McGraw-Hill, New York.

- Van Oech, R (1990) A Whack on the Side of the Head, Warner Books, New York.

- Viorst, J (1986) Alexander and the Terrible, Horrible, No Good, Very Bad Day, Angus and Roberston, North Ryde.

- Waitley, D (1983) Seeds of Greatness, Old Tappan, New Jersey.

- Ziglar, Z (1991) See You at the Top, Pelica, Gretna.